The Lawyer's *Quick* Guide To Timeslips®

American Bar Association
Law Practice Management Section

Defending Liberty
Pursuing Justice

Cover design by Samuel Girton.

Nothing contained in this book is to be considered as the rendering of legal advice for specific cases, and readers are responsible for obtaining such advice from their own legal counsel. This book and any forms and agreements herein are intended for educational and informational purposes only.

The products and services mentioned in this publication are under or may be under trademark or service mark protection. Product and service names and terms are used throughout only in an editorial fashion, to the benefit of the product manufacturer or service provider, with no intention of infringement. Use of a product or service name or term in this publication should not be regarded as affecting the validity of any trademark or service mark.

The Section of Law Practice Management, American Bar Association, offers an educational program for lawyers in practice. Books and other materials are published in furtherance of that program. Authors and editors of publications may express their own legal interpretations and opinions, which are not necessarily those of either the American Bar Association or the Section of Law Practice Management unless adopted pursuant to the By-laws of the Association. The opinions expressed do not reflect in any way a position of the Section or the American Bar Association.

© 1998 American Bar Association. All rights reserved.
Printed in the United States of America.

Library of Congress Catalog Card Number 98-72615
ISBN 1-57073-587-5

02 01 00 99 98   5 4 3 2 1

Discounts are available for books ordered in bulk. Special consideration is given to state bars, CLE programs, and other bar-related organizations. Inquire at Book Publishing, American Bar Association, 750 N. Lake Shore Drive, Chicago, Illinois 60611.

Table of Contents

About the Author vii
Acknowledgments ix
Foreword xi

Introduction   1
    What Timeslips Does   2
    What Timeslips Doesn't Do   2
    About this Book   2
    What's New in Version 7   4
    What's New in Version 8   6
    A Note about Version 9   6
    Conventions Used   7
    Using the Navigator   8
    What to Do First   9
    Where to Go from Here   9

Chapter One: Lesson 1: Entering Time Slips   11
    Exiting TSTimer   20
    TSTimer Shortcuts   20
    Where to Go from Here   21

Chapter Two: Lesson 2: Entering Disbursements   23
    Creating a New Expense Activity Code   25
    Other Things You Might Want to Know
        About Entering Slips   30

Chapter Three: Lesson 3: Entering Payment Transactions   37
    About the Browse Transaction Screen   41
    Other Transaction Types and When to Use Them   41

Chapter Four: The Billing Cycle   45
    Lawyers' Overview of the Billing Cycle   45
    Getting More Information from Timeslips: Reports Overview   51

Billing Tips and Tricks   52
More Stuff about Reports   55
Daily Time Report   56
Relative and Absolute Dates   60
Charges on Hold   62
Billing Worksheets   63
Making Corrections with and without the Billing Assistant   67
Backing Up Your Data   72
Printing Bills   72
Printing Procedure and Proof Stage   80
Proof Stage   82
Revision Stage   84
Finalizing Bills   84
Undo Finalized Bills   86
Reprinting Bills   87
Conclusion   89

Chapter Five: Getting More Professional-Looking Bills — 91
Bill Layout   91
Bill Format   92
Sort and Option Screens   92
Time and Expense Slips   93
Changing Your Billing Layout   93
Font Settings   96
Phrases   96
Order and Attributes   96
Details for Preparing Sample Bills   98

Chapter Six: Special Handling: Flat Fees and Retainers — 105
Flat Fees and Monthly Retainers   109
Getting Information to Help You Analyze Your Retainers
    and Flat Fees   111

Chapter Seven: Setting Up Timeslips — 113
Create a New Database   113
Terminology   113
Update Capacity   114
Operational Preferences   115
Billing Rates   115
Key Clients and the Options for Handling Clients and Matters   116
Personal Preferences   118
Security   119
Financial Rules   120

Create Attorney Nicknames and Rates   120
Create Activity Codes   122
Task-Based Billing Considerations   122
Entering Time Activity Nicknames   124
Entering Disbursement Activity Codes   126
Custom Client Fields   128
How to Create Custom Client Fields   129
Abbreviations   131
Setting Up Clients   133
Company Address and Client Defaults   134
Attaching Custom Client Fields to Client's Information Screen   134
Tax, Interest & Markup   135
Bill Format 1 And 2   135
Bill Format 2   136
Override Client Rates   138

Appendix A: Shortcut Keys 141

Appendix B: Basic Procedures Checklist for Timeslips Deluxe for Windows 145

Appendix C: Timeslips Reports 147

Index 157

About the Author

Carol L. Schlein is an attorney and President of Law Office Systems, Inc., a New York City area technology training and consulting firm. She is a former member of the Council of the Law Practice Management Section of the American Bar Association and former chair of its Computer and Technology Division. Ms. Schlein is a Certified Consultant on Timeslips®, timekeeping and billing software, a Certified Resource on WordPerfect®, an Independent Authorized Consultant on Time Matters® legal case management software and a Certified Consultant on Amicus Attorney®. She writes a monthly question and answer column on technology for the *New Jersey Lawyer* and has designed and conducted computer training classes for members of the New Jersey State Bar Association. Ms. Schlein is a frequent lecturer on topics of law office automation for the American Bar Association, the New York State Bar Association, the New Jersey State Bar Association and other organizations. Carol Schlein earned a B.A. in Political Science from the University of Rochester, a J.D. from New York Law School, and is admitted to practice in New York.

Acknowledgments

In developing, creating and editing this book, I want to thank the following people for their support, influence, and for beleaguering me to finish the book. I especially appreciate the efforts of my husband, Craig MacCallum, and my daughter, Margaret MacCallum in putting up with me; my assistant, Lee Jefferies for her input, ideas, and creative editing; and Mitch Russo and Matt Lafata of SAGE US for their encouragement and assistance in making this book technically accurate. Special thanks to the incredible group of Timeslips Certified Consultants, particularly Carolyn MacKenzie and the New York TSUTIL group for their inspiration, encouragement, advice and support. I also appreciate the encouragement and continual feedback from my clients over the years that went into the development of the book. I would also like to thank the ABA Section of Law Practice Management Publishing Board and publishing staff who have kept me from giving up on this project many times.

Foreword

In 1991, the ABA Law Practice Management Section released what quickly became one of its best-selling publications, *WordPerfect in One Hour for Lawyers,* by Gerald Robinson. That handy little manual for WordPerfect 5.1 for DOS users sold thousands of copies to lawyers ready to put the power of computers to work on their own desks. LPM Publishing followed that book with Carol Schlein's *WordPerfect Shortcuts for Lawyers: Learning Merge and Macros in One Hour,* and our popular "In One Hour" series was launched. It now includes books on Quicken, HotDocs and Microsoft Word for Windows.

In addition to the In One Hour books, featuring four 15-minute lessons to enable lawyers to learn basic software operations, LPM Publishing has released the "Lawyer's Quick Guide" series. "Quick Guides" enable you to learn the basics of more complex software applications that do not lend themselves to the In One Hour format, but which lawyers can profitably use without having to master advanced features. This series includes such works as Burgess Allison's *The Lawyer's Quick Guides to Netscape Navigator* and *Microsoft Internet Explorer,* and David Greenwald's and Guy Wiggins' *The Lawyer's Quick Guide to WordPerfect 7.0/8.0 for Windows.*

We are pleased to offer Carol Schlein's second work for LPM Publishing, *The Lawyer's Quick Guide to Timeslips®* (versions 7.0 and 8.0). Ms. Schlein, a computer consultant and trainer, has produced an easy-to-use handbook for learning the basic features of the popular Timeslips Deluxe for Windows time and billing program. Although the majority of Timeslips users are lawyers who want to enter their own time as they work or their billing staff, the Timeslips manual and tutorial are not focused on the unique needs of law firms. This book walks you through the program so that you can record your time, track expenses and payments, customize your bills, track what clients owe and analyze the financial performance of your law office and its timekeepers. You will also learn how to use Timeslips with your word processing, case management and document management programs.

This book is intended for lawyers who want to enter their own time and make use of the useful features of Timeslips, lawyers who want to understand better the features and limitations of the program, and law office staff who enter and maintain timekeeping information and prepare time and billing reports. You will learn how to set up the Timeslips program to best ensure that you are taking advantage of the most helpful features and shortcuts; enter time records; keep track of disbursements; record payment transactions; produce reports for time, disbursement details, transactions, charges on hold, full detail billing worksheets, billing worksheet summaries, and final bills. Ms. Schlein also gives you helpful tips so that you do not unconsciously sabotage your implementation of Timeslips by focusing on the wrong details or creating too many exceptions and not enough rules. You will also learn how to make your bills look more professional, and how to handle special needs such as flat fees and retainers. Appendices give you shortcuts, and a checklist for basic procedures, and a summary of the more than 50 reports Timeslips can generate to help you analyze your financial picture.

LPM Publishing's In One Hour and Quick Guide series are offered so that you can avoid reading hundreds of manual pages or attending lengthy seminars. We hope that this book proves to be as beneficial as its predecessors in enabling you to learn basic software skills quickly.

> Robert J. Conroy
> Judith L. Grubner
> Co-Chairs, LPM Publishing

Introduction

TIMESLIPS DELUXE FOR WINDOWS is a superb time and billing program for sole practitioners and lawyers in small and medium-sized firms. It can even be used by renegade lawyers in large firms who want to enter their own time in the computer as they work. Busy lawyers and their staffs are sometimes reluctant to invest the time necessary to learn the proper way to use the program and apply it to their practices. While the majority of Timeslips users are lawyers, the program is also used by other professionals. Consequently, the manual and tutorial that accompany the program do not focus solely on the unique needs of law offices. This book is intended to remedy that situation. If you have struggled with the program, you know that it can be difficult to master and use effectively. If you have not, it could be because you have left it sitting unopened on your shelf or have made compromises about how your clients get billed or what information appears on those bills.

What Timeslips Does

Timeslips's strength is in enabling you to record your time as you do your work. You can also use it to track expenses and payments and prepare customized bills to send to your clients. It can assist you in tracking how much they owe and provides tools to analyze the financial performance of your firm, its clients, and timekeepers.

Timeslips Corporation also sells add-on utilities including Speller, which can be used to proofread the text of your slips, and TAL, the Timeslips Accounting Link, which lets Timeslips track payments by invoice. TAL allows you to track fees and expenses separately, and can transfer transactions (payment information) and invoices to one of thirty different accounting programs.

What Timeslips Doesn't Do

Timeslips does not do Windows! Just kidding. Actually, in its use of graphics, Timeslips Corporation is the most experienced of the main legal time and billing vendors. Prior to its first Windows version, Timeslips already had a version of the program for the Apple Macintosh environment. It has now done four Windows versions and is ahead of its competitors in taking advantage of the graphical environment.

By itself, Timeslips does not provide all the management tools a modern law firm requires. It does not handle case management, document management, or word processing. It does, however, work well with a number of programs that do perform those tasks and can share information with them.

About this Book

This book has been organized to allow you to learn quickly the concepts and basic steps involved in using Timeslips for Windows in a law office. It is written with three different types of people in mind: the lawyer who is not a hands-on user of the program but wants to understand better the capabilities and limitations of the program; the lawyer who is a hands-on user and wants to enter his or her own time and wants to understand the program in greater detail; and the staff that maintains the information in the program and oversees the billing process. This last group needs to have a more complete understanding of how the different components of the program fit together. Where the needs of the three groups coincide, there is general information. Where the staff requires different information from the lawyers interested in an overview, the overview precedes the detailed instructions.

If you want a general overview, you can skim the book. You should focus on the options available in each section so you can better guide your staff to streamline their use of the program. I hope you'll be inspired to move to the next level: a hands-on user. To enter your own Timeslips, spend some time with Lesson One and your computer.

To get your money's worth from the program, once you are entering your own slips, read through Chapter 7, "Setting Up Timeslips," to ensure that you are taking advantage of all of the shortcuts and features.

If you are a do-it-your-selfer or are the billing person in your office, start with Setting Up Timeslips and then read the rest of the book in order. Do not overlook this section and the appendices as they include tips and tricks based on years of experience working with Timeslips and small law offices.

Many law offices are still using earlier versions of Timeslips. To a great extent, the instructions included in this book also work in prior versions. Where the features are only available in Version 7 or 8, they are noted.

There are many ways that Timeslips can be customized for a law-firm environment. These are explained in detail in Chapter 7. Among the features you can customize are the labels for the main components of your time entry screen. We will refer to the lawyers whose time is recorded as either "Attorney" or "Timekeeper." The Timeslips manual refers to them as "User." Similarly, the label for Client can also be changed. We will refer to this interchangeably as either Client, Case, or Matter in our discussion. Beginning on page 118 there is an extensive discussion about the different ways to set up clients and their matters. You should review this before doing any serious data entry in the program. Finally, the Activity field, which is used for time and expense codes, can also be changed. We'll stick to Activity when referring to this field.

When you install Timeslips, you are actually installing several programs at once. In Windows 3.X, they will install as a Program Group. In Windows 95, you will see a list of options below Timeslips Deluxe under Programs. Figure 1 shows the icons that are installed in Windows.

TSReport is the main Timeslips program itself and includes access to the Timer, Bill Layout, Script Editor, and Navigator Editor.

TSTimer is another way to enter time and disbursement slips. This option takes you directly into Make Slips.

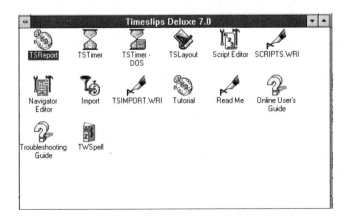

FIGURE 1. Timeslips Deluxe Program Group as it appears in Windows 3.X

TSTimer DOS is a holdover for people on older computers or those who prefer the faster entry available through the DOS time and expense entry screen (Make Slips).

TSLayout is the tool you use to edit your Bill Layout.

Script Editor is used to create new and modify existing scripts, which are attached to buttons on the Navigator to perform functions within Timeslips. This tool is usually used only by advanced users and should be used carefully.

SCRIPTS.WRI is the help instructions for using the Script Editor.

Navigator Editor is used to edit the buttons on the different panels of the Navigator. You can edit the Navigator directly from inside Timeslips by selecting TOOLS/Edit Navigator.

Import is used to bring client information or slip information from other sources into Timeslips.

TSIMPORT.WRI is the help instructions for importing data into Timeslips.

Tutorial gives you access to the sample database along with a special Navigator and associated scripts that guide you through the basic functions of the program.

Readme provides last-minute changes to the program that the manufacturer wants you to know about before using the program.

Online User's Guide and **Troubleshooting Guide** are intended to assist you when you have questions. You can get to either of these resources directly through Help within TSReport.

What's New in Version 7

People who upgrade from one version of a program to another often miss or ignore the new features in order to keep productivity in their office at the same level. Ironically, in doing this, they often miss better ways to perform tasks. Generally, I advise people that if they feel like they are doing something the long way, they should find out how to do it faster and easier. You can also assume that if you have been frustrated by a program's inability to handle a particular function, you are not alone and can expect subsequent versions of the program to address the shortcoming.

If you are upgrading from an older version of Timeslips, there are a few features you should explore and integrate into your firm's procedures:

- The **Billing Assistant** was added in Version 6. This lets you visually edit your bills before you print them. Instead of having to change slips in Make Slips and client information in Browse Client Information, you can jump to them through the Billing Assistant.

You can establish **Slip Defaults** in Make Slips. You can set Timeslips so that it will automatically repeat information from the previous slip. This can save a lot of time when entering information.

- The **List View** in Make Slips lets you look at or edit selected slips in a list format. This is ideal for the attorney who jumps back and forth among a small group of slips each day and keeps adding time to them. You can also now print the slips that have been selected through the List view of Make Slips in the Detail Report format for easier proofreading and backup. The timer has also been enhanced to allow you to attach a bookmark to specific slips. You can then use the GoTo function to jump quickly to your bookmarks.
- Timeslips 7 added the option to **Close Slips** rather than purge and archive them. This is an improvement that lets you access specific slips when necessary. Unlike purge and archive, through Closed Slips you can select which client and what date range you want to view.
- Timeslips 7 added the ability to make clients hidden **(Clients, Hidden).** By designating a client as hidden, you remove it from the list of active clients when making selections for slips, reports, and bills. The client's information is still in the system but it is invisible. If, however, you need to include hidden clients, you need to unhide them to return them to active status before you can access their information.
- The **Report Wizard** is a tool that lets you specify which information you would like to see in a report from the system and have Timeslips determine which report matches your need. Through a series of questions, Report Wizard narrows your criteria and guides you to the best available report. Pay careful attention to the choices you make so you can duplicate the report again in the future, especially if you like the resulting report. You may also want to take a look at the overview of the available reports, which starts on page 51, and Appendix C, which lists and briefly explains each of the available reports.
- **Description Abbreviations** have been enhanced so that you can design abbreviations that pause for additional information. For instance, you may prefer to describe your telephone calls as "Telephone call with John Smith, Esq., regarding . . . " In previous versions, you could either set up two separate abbreviations (one for "telephone call with" and the other for, "Esq., regarding") or

use a single code and type the remaining portion of the description. In Version 7, you can insert a prompt within a single abbreviation so that you can add the opposing attorney's name. This means there are much fewer abbreviations to memorize, while you can provide your client with more detail and fewer typos.
- In addition to rate tables associated with the timekeepers, clients, and activities, you can also establish **Override Rates.** These rates can be defined for specific circumstances. For instance, you might have a special rate for an initial client consultation that is different from normal rates or you might have a special rate when the lawyer is in court. You can set up a rule list that can be associated with individual clients.
- The **Bill Layout** program has been enhanced in several significant ways for lawyers. You can now create a customized cover page or summary page. You have more fields that you can insert into the cover pages or onto the bill itself. For example, you can enter text that says "For Professional Services Rendered" and follow it by the codes for starting and ending dates, resulting in a phrase that includes the date range used to select the slips for the actual bill. Prior to this version, many firms had to do a significant amount of work to get a similar result, particularly when the date ranges differed from client to client in the same billing cycle. You also have more flexibility when using a consolidated bill for clients with multiple matters.

What's New in Version 8

As this book is being finished, Version 8 has just been released. The first thing you will notice about Version 8 is that many of the dialogs and pull-down buttons have been replaced by the tabbed views popular in many Windows 95-based products. You can also now use the right mouse button to access relevant commands.

By and large, since this book is intended to help you learn the basics, most of the functions and steps described here are still applicable. The most dramatic change is the addition of the Revision Stage. In Versions 6 and 7, after you printed your bills and placed them on Proof Stage, you could either finalize them or clear them from Proof Stage. This meant you would have to reconstruct all the appropriate settings (date range for slips and transactions) for that revised bill. Revision Stage collects that information while allowing you to make changes before reprocessing a bill.

Other additions to Version 8 include:

- Can enter Billable and Do Not Bill time on a single slip and track the adjustment (Do Not Bill time will not print on your bill);
- Can attach bold, underline, or italics to slips descriptions;
- Better functionality in a network environment;
- Can perform conflict-of-interest checking and improved text searching of information entered in Timeslips.

A Note about Version 9

As this book is going to press, Version 9, the first 32-bit edition of Timeslips, is being released. Please refer to the Timeslips Web site at **www.timeslips.com** for all the details.

Conventions Used

Writing instructions for Windows-based programs has become a challenge. Some people prefer to use the keyboard and keyboard shortcuts while others glue their fingers to their mouse. All of the functions of the program are available through the pull-down menus across the top of the screen. To access these, you can use the mouse or the keyboard. Using the mouse, you would click on the menu title to display the pull-down menu options. You can then highlight the option you want with the mouse and click on it to select it. If you prefer to use the keyboard, hold down the **ALT** key and press the underlined letter associated with the menu item you want. You can then press the underlined letter connected with the menu option you want. You do not need to press the **ALT** key again once the pull-down menu is displayed. You could also use the up and down arrow keys to select an option from the pull-down menu.

Since many of the steps will require you to select from a main menu, then a submenu, and sometimes go one or two other levels deep, we have developed a shortcut for indicating the levels. Rather than explain that you select Settings from the Main Menu, then select Custom Text from the Settings Menu, and finally Abbreviations from the Custom Text Submenu, we will abbreviate those steps as follows:

SETTINGS/Custom Text/Abbreviations

Timeslips adds a third option for selecting program functions. The Navigator is an icon-based representation of many of the functions of the program.

Using the Navigator

Three Navigators ship with the program: Basic, Advanced, and Guided Tour. To switch among the navigators, choose TOOLS/Use Navigator and select the one you want. Unless you like to be tortured, stick with the Basic Navigator. It has fewer buttons than the Advanced one. Figure 2 shows the Basic Navigator that comes with Version 7 of Timeslips Deluxe. Version 6 does not include a button on the Bill Cycle panel for Pre-Bill (Full Detail) Worksheets, but this could be added back in by using the Navigator Editor.

> ➤TIP: If your Navigator isn't showing or disappears, press **CTRL+F10** or Select HELP/Navigator to redisplay it. You can make sure it always shows when you start the program by selecting SETTINGS/Preferences/View: Navigator and Script Options, then Click on Yes for "Show Navigator on start-up."

Each button within a panel is controlled by a script written by Timeslips Corporation. These scripts automate steps related to their functions. Often, they include a few more steps than the pull-down menu version. If you want to customize your copy of Timeslips, you can either learn to write your own scripts (not a task I would recommend) or hire a Timeslips Certified Consultant to assist you in the task.

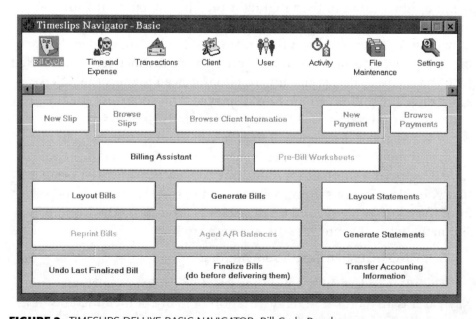

FIGURE 2. TIMESLIPS DELUXE BASIC NAVIGATOR: Bill Cycle Panel

The Navigator consists of eight panels: Bill Cycle, Time and Expense, Transactions, Client, User, Activity, File Maintenance, and Settings. Each panel of the Navigator is intended to group the tasks related to that particular aspect of the program. For example, the File Maintenance panel includes functions used in maintaining your database such as backing up, accessing other databases, and so on.

The **Bill Cycle** panel is where you will spend most of your time once you have finished the basic setup of the program. Buttons include New or Browse Slips, Browse Client Information, New or Browse Payments, Billing Assistant, and Generate Bills. Several of the buttons on this panel are the same as buttons on the other panels but are placed here since they relate to steps involved in the billing cycle.

The **Time and Expense** panel focuses its buttons on managing slips.

The **Transactions** panel includes buttons for entering and working with payments, adjustments, and credits.

The **Client** panel includes buttons for managing client information and printing client-based reports.

The **User (Attorney)** panel has buttons for entering attorney nicknames and rates and creating reports based on the attorneys' efforts.

The **Activity** panel is similar to the Attorney and Client panels but focuses on time and expense codes.

The **File Maintenance** panel has most of the administrative functions, such as creating and changing databases and importing and purging tools.

The **Settings** panel contains the buttons required for doing preliminary setup to Timeslips for general use.

What to Do First

If you are new to the program you must set up the attorneys, your clients, and billing codes. (Start with Setting Up Clients (page 133), which walks you through most of the setup issues.) A convenient check list of where to find the steps required for setting up and using Timeslips in your law office can be found on pages 10-12.

Where to Go from Here

The ability to time your work as you do it has been shown to be one of the most cost-effective uses of technology a law firm can embrace.

What to Do	Menu Steps to Start	Page
BASIC SETUP		
Create a new database	FILE/New	
Change labels (Terminology)	SETTINGS/Terminology	
Update Capacity	FILE/Update Capacity	
Set Client Defaults (Operational Preferences)	SETTINGS/Operational	
Define Attorney Nicknames and Billing Rates	NAMES/Attorney Information (**CTRL + U**)	
Define Time Activity Codes	NAMES/Activity Information (**CTRL + Y**)	
Define Disbursement (Expense) Activity Codes	NAMES/Activity Information (**CTRL + Y**)	
Define Custom Client Fields	SETTINGS/Custom Fields	
Enter time description Abbreviations	SETTINGS/Custom Text/ Abbreviations	
Design Bill Layout	BILLS/Generate Bills/Template/ Open	
Enter Client Information (nicknames, addresses, re, custom client fields, previous balance and bill format)	NAMES/Client Information (**CTRL + I**)	
Daily Activities		
Enter Time slips	SLIPS/Make Slips (**CTRL + M**)	
Enter Expense slips	SLIPS/Make Slips (**CTRL + M**)	
Enter Payments (Transactions)	NAMES/Client Transactions (**CTRL + T**)	
Print Daily Time Report (optional)	REPORTS/Slip Analysis/ User Defined	

What to Do	*Menu Steps to Start*	*Page*
BACKUP! BACKUP! BACKUP!!!		
End of Month Activities		
Print Charges on Hold Report	REPORTS/2 Client WIP/Charges on Hold	
Print Transactions or Payments Report	REPORT/1 Client Transaction Listing	
Print Full Detail Pre-Billing Worksheets	BILLS/Pre-bill Worksheets/ Full Detail (**CTRL + F**)	
Use Billing Assistant to make corrections	BILLS/Billing Assistant	
BACKUP!!!		
Print Bills to File—do not finalize (recommended)	BILLS/Generate Bills or **CTRL + B**/Output to File	
Print Bills to Printer	BILLS/Generate Bills or **CTRL + B**/ Output to Printer	
Place Bills on Proof Stage	BILLS/Generate Bills or **CTRL + B** after generation select Proof Stage from Generation of Bills Completed dialog box	
Change Bills to Revision Stage (Ver 8) or remove from Proof Stage (Ver 7) or Undo Bill (earlier) to correct individual bills	BILLS/Bills in Proof Stage select Clear (Ver 6 and 7)	
Finalize Bills with Billing Summary Worksheet selected under Options	BILLS/Finalize Bills	
Perform Finalization Backup	BILLS/Finalize Bills select Yes on Finalization dialog box	
End of Month Reports		
Accounts Receivable	REPORTS/1 Client/Accounts Receivable	

What to Do	Menu Steps to Start	Page
Client List (optional)	REPORTS/1 Client/Name & Address Listing	
End of Year / Periodic Activities		
Close Slips	SLIPS/Close Slips	
Hide Clients	NAMES/Client Info/Hidden	
Client History Report	REPORTS/History Listing	
User Report—Overall History	REPORTS/User/Overall History	
Purge Billed Transactions	FILE/Purge/Yes/Transactions	

Forgetting to record a single ten-minute phone call seems minor until you multiply it by five days per week, twenty days per month, and so on. Suddenly, losing ten or fifteen minutes of billable time per day is no longer trivial.

The pop-up timer, while enhanced over the years, has been a part of the Timeslips product since its first version. Only in recent years, however, have most lawyers put a computer on their desks. Many lawyers still have not used Timeslips to record their time as they work.

It is clearly worth the investment to have the lawyers in your firm learn to enter their own time. It will be more complete and more accurate since there is no hand writing to misinterpret, and it will streamline the billing cycle since there will be no data-entry bottleneck at the end of the month. Assuming someone has already set up your firm's attorneys, clients, and activity codes (if not, start with Chapter 7, "Setting Up Timeslips"), Lesson One will get you up and timing!

CHAPTER **ONE**

Lesson 1: Entering Time Slips

OBJECTIVE: TO ENTER YOUR TIME directly into Timeslips as you work.

We have assumed that your firm has already completed the basic setup including defining attorneys and their rates, activity codes for time and expenses, and basic client information. If not, read the Introduction and start with Chapter 7: Setting Up Timeslips, which reviews the steps required to set up and customize the program. We have also assumed you have read the introduction to this book and are familiar with the main components of Timeslips and have already seen the Navigator.

As with all Windows-based programs, there are many ways to perform the same functions. We will focus on the simplest method and then discuss the other options. The fancy steps and some tips and tricks are at the end of each chapter.

Your first task is to get to the TSTimer screen (see Figure 3). If you are using Windows 3.X and you have an icon on your Windows Program Manager for TSTimer, you should double-click on it. If you are using Windows 95, and there isn't a TSTimer icon on your desktop or at the top of the START Menu, choose Start/Programs/Timeslips Deluxe/TSTimer.

If you do not have an icon for TSTimer, double-click on the TSReport icon. If you prefer to use the keyboard, from the TSReport screen you can press **CTRL+M.** If you like to use the pull-down menus, select SLIPS/Make Slips, or if you like using the Navigator, highlight the Bill Cycle Panel (if it isn't already highlighted) and click on Browse Slips or New Slip.

If you do not have an icon labeled either TSTimer or TSReport, follow whatever steps your office has established to get you into Timeslips and then follow one of the options above for getting to the Slips screen.

The Lawyer's Quick Guide to Timeslips®

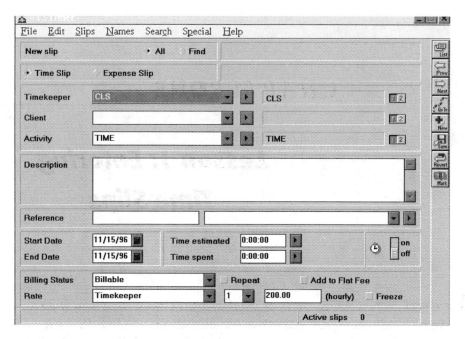

FIGURE 3. TSTimer Screen: New Slip

1. Unless you selected New Slip from the Navigator, you need to start a new slip. The fastest way to do this is to hold down the **CTRL** key and tap the letter **N**. (If you really hate to use the keyboard, you can use your mouse to click on the **NEW** button on the right-hand side of the screen.) (See Figure 4.)

   Once you have told Timeslips to start a new slip, you are ready to enter the information.

FIGURE 4. New Button, Part of Tool Icons on Right Hand Side of TSTimer Screen

2. **Attorney (User) Nickname:** Type part or all of your Attorney's Nickname unless it is already displayed on the screen. As you begin to type, you will see your nickname appear. When you see your nickname, you can press the **TAB** key to move to the next field or use the mouse to click into the Client Field.

If your nickname doesn't appear, you can look for it on the list of available nicknames by clicking the down triangle (▼) or press **F4** with your mouse. If your name is on that list, click on it to select it. Timeslips allows you to identify your timekeepers with two different nicknames. If the nicknames available from the list do not look familiar, try clicking on the number 1 or 2 button to the right of the nickname field to display the alternate set of nicknames. (See Figure 5)

If it is still not there, then we have to assume your firm hasn't done any basic setup yet. While we could let you cheat (since you could enter all these codes on the fly), you'll be better off in the long run if you systematically go through Chapter 7: Setting up Timeslips. You'll also find it much easier to learn how to enter your time if you aren't also learning how to set up the system at the same time.

FIGURE 5. Button to Switch between Nickname One and Two

3. **Starting the Timer:** Once you have identified yourself as the timekeeper for the slip, you can actually start to time your work. To do this, press **CTRL** and tap the letter **T**. (Keyboard phobics can click on any part of the **On/Off** button near the lower right-hand corner of the time entry screen.) Take a look at Figure 6 which shows the time spent increasing with the **On/Off** switch next to it.
4. **Client Nickname:** Type part or all of the Client's (or case) Nickname until you see it appear in the field. If you have a lot of clients with similar nicknames, you may want to click the down triangle (▼) or press the **F4** key to pop up the list of available codes. Click on the client's nickname whose work you are doing

FIGURE 6. Timer on; on/off Button in on Position

and it will be inserted into the field. Use the **TAB** key to move to the next field or click in the next field with your mouse.

5. **Activity Code:** Type part or all of the Activity Code for the work you are doing. If you have followed my suggestion in the setup section, you can type **T - I - M - E** or enough of the code until it appears in the field. If you are using Timeslips in conjunction with a case-management program, try to use the same activity description codes for both programs. If you need to prepare task-based bills, you will need to know the appropriate activity code for the task you are performing. Use the **TAB** key to move to the next field or click in the next field with your mouse.

6. **Description of Work:** Type the full text description for the work you are doing or have done.

    If your firm has used one of the predefined installation options or has set up its own abbreviation codes, you can select those from a list by pressing **F7** or choose **EDIT/Abbreviations** from the pull-down menu when your cursor is in the Description field. If you already know your firm's abbreviations, you can type the letters of the abbreviation. When you press the space bar or add punctuation such as a period, comma, semicolon, or colon, you will see your abbreviation expand. If you are using Version 7, you might get a prompt on the screen first asking you to insert text within the abbreviation.

You can also add new abbreviations as you need them by pressing the **F7** key to call up the list and then selecting **NEW** to create a new abbreviation. See page 131 for instructions about setting up abbreviations.

> ►TIPS: Most of the general Windows cursor movements and text-entry issues work here. Use **HOME** to move the cursor to left margin. Use **END** to move the cursor to the end of text near right margin. You can also use **CTRL+←** or **CTRL+→** to move the cursor from word to word. You can also use the mouse to highlight text you want to eliminate. Unlike your word processor, though, you cannot click and drag and do fancy editing here. Highlighted text can be deleted by typing replacement text, so be careful! **CTRL+Z** will let you undo any mistakes.

Use the **TAB** key to move to the next field or click in the next field with your mouse.

7. **Reference:** The Reference field should be completed *Only* if your firm is using it for Matters, for task-based information, or for sorting purposes. If you are skipping the reference field, use

the **TAB** key to move to the Start Date field or click your mouse on the Start Date field. If you are not sure you are using Matters, you can check to see if any have been entered for your client by clicking on the down triangle (▼). You may also want to review the discussion about how to set up your clients and matters beginning on page 133.

To enter Matters directly, type an * (asterisk) before the Timeslips assigned matter number. If you are unsure which matter number to use, click on the down triangle (▼) or press **F4** to search the list of existing matters, highlight the desired matter, and click on it to select it.

8. **Start Date (From Date** in earlier versions**):** Unless you have customized your preferences, Timeslips should already have today's date in the Start Date field and the same date in the End Date field. If so, you can move directly to the Time Spent field. You'll find that you can't get there if you have the Timer running, so be sure to turn the Timer off first. To turn the Timer off, press **CTRL** and tap the letter **T** or click your mouse on any part of the On/Off button near the lower right-hand corner of your time entry screen.

   If the date is wrong, you can type a correct one using the format ***mmddyy.*** There are a few neat shortcuts you can use to put the correct date into the slip:

- Type **T** to insert TODAY'S DATE, or
- Highlight the Start Date field and type the *number* of the day in the current month (e.g., if you enter 3, it will translate that to the third of the current month), or
- Press the plus or minus sign to bring up a dialog box that lets you add or subtract days from today.

In Version 7, when you are entering dates, you will see a calendar icon (See Figure 7) next to both date fields.

When you are in time or disbursement entry or entering transactions, clicking on the calendar icon or pressing **F9** will display a calendar that looks like Figure 8.

| Start Date | 11/15/96 |
| End Date | 11/15/96 |

FIGURE 7. Calendar Icon for Start and End Date Fields

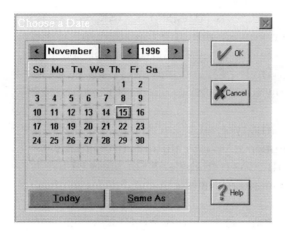

FIGURE 8. TSTimer Calendar

You can click on the arrows to the left or right of the month to move forward or backward a month a time. You can do the same thing with the arrows surrounding the year. You can also click on a day in the displayed month to select that date. At the bottom, it gives you the options for Today and Same As. You would use "same as" for the End Date field.

In other parts of the program, such as the Select screen when you are preparing bills and reports, you will get a fancier calendar that includes tabs for Relative and Actual dates. Actual dates are ones that are set in stone. If you set the actual date as July 4th and save the settings as a screen, it will remain July 4th the next time you retrieve those settings. Relative dates are relative to whatever today's date happens to be. You can select from choices such as "Last Month," "Last Week," and so on. When you use a screen that has been stored with Relative dates, Timeslips will look at today's date and determine what date you intend based on that selection. This is generally used by more-advanced users of the program for programming scripts and is beyond the scope of this book.

9. **End Date (Thru Date** in earlier versions**):** Move the cursor to the End Date and type **S** to make it the same as the Start Date.
10. **Time Spent:** There are a number of different ways to enter the amount of time you worked into Timeslips. As you already saw, you could use the timer. This is one of the main benefits of Timeslips since it allows you to enter your time as you do your work. By recording your work as you do it, you can be more accurate and will probably track more time than you would account for on paper or after the fact.

a. To record your time in tenths of an hour: type **hr.tenths** (e.g. 2.2, .4, etc.) On the screen, the time will be converted to minutes. In reports, it will revert back to tenths or another amount depending upon how you set up your clients' rounding options, or

b. To record time in hours and minutes: type **hr:min** (e.g. 2:20, :05, etc.), or

c. Press **S** in the Time Spent field to bring up the Time Range dialog box (see Figure 9). This will let you enter the time of day that you started and ended your work for a client and have Timeslips calculate how long you spent.

If you use Start and Stop times, the next slip you create will assume your new starting time is the ending time from the previous slip. This helps you account for all of your time during the day. This option is ideal for lawyers who tend to work in big time blocks on individual projects.

11. **Billing Status Options:** Most of the work you do will be Billable and charged at your normal billing rate or the rate you set up for this client. If the options at the bottom appear to be correct, you are ready to save your slip.

Occasionally, some of the work you do will not be billable to the client. Timeslips gives you several other choices that are explained in the chart on page 21.

12. **Saving Your Slip:** When you are finished entering your slip, you are ready to save it. Press **CTRL+S** or click on the **Save** button on the right-hand side of the screen.

When you save the slip, Timeslips will attach a slip number to the slip and will show you the value (rate times hours) of the slip just above the attorney's name.

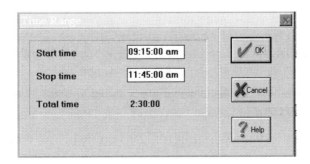

FIGURE 9. Start/Stop Time Dialog Screen

Whew!! You've now entered your first slip. If you want to start a new slip immediately, you can click the **New** button or press **CTRL+N** to start the new slip and save the one that was on your screen.

➤Version 8 Note: After you have saved a slip, Timeslips calculates the value of the slip based on the amount of time and the billing rate. When you click on the value in the upper right-hand corner, you can make additional adjustments, including the ability to write off part of the time or dollars of the slip as "Do Not Bill." This is ideal if an associate has spent too long on a task and you do not want the client to see the actual time spent. However, be forewarned that the client will not see this type of adjustment reflected on his bill although this adjustment will be included in analysis reports and on the billing worksheet.

Exiting TSTimer

If you are going to continue with the next lesson, you should stay in TSTimer.

When you are ready to exit TSTimer, you should select **F**ile/Exit or press **ALT+F4.** If you are using Windows 3.X, you can double-click on the control bar (the little minus sign in the upper left-hand corner of the screen) to exit this window. If you are using Windows 95, you can click on the X in the upper right-hand corner to exit this window.

If you got to TSTimer through TSReport, you will return to TSReport. You can exit it following the same options to exit TSTimer described above.

➤TIPS: Be sure someone backs up your work every day. If you like to review your work while it is fresh in your mind, consider printing a Detail Report for your time slips every day. You can do this directly from the List View of TSTimer or from the Reports pull-down menu.

If you prefer a clearer format, refer to the steps for creating a "Daily Time Report," in Chapter 4, "The Billing Cycle."

TSTimer Shortcuts

There are a few shortcuts you might like to know before you enter more slips:

CTRL+D	Duplicate Slip	Used to duplicate the *entire* slip. You can then edit the new slips for specific changes such as a different client or different price or quantity.
F8	Duplicate (Clone) Field	Used to duplicate the field from the previously displayed slip into the slip you are creating.
ALT+F8	Duplicate (Clone) Rest	Used to duplicate all fields from the previously displayed slip from your cursor location to the end of the slip.

Where to Go from Here

At the end of the Lesson on Disbursement Entry is a section that explains many of the other features available in the TSTimer portion of the program for both time and expense slips. If you are recording your time directly into the program, you should review those capabilities with special attention to the MiniView and the Slip List.

BILLING STATUS OPTIONS

Status Option	When to Use	Impact on Bill
Billable	For slips that get charged to the client including clients with flat fees.	Hours and amount from slip will be added to total. Part of work in progress until billed and finalized.
Hold	Do not use if possible. It is better to put entire client or matter on hold than individual slips.	Slip will not be included on bill even if client is billed and the bill is finalized. Use Charges on Hold report to monitor.
No Charge	For work that you have done that you want the client to see on the bill.	Text of slip will appear on the bill; hours will be added but amount will *not* be added to total. "No Charge" will appear to the right of the slip description. Amounts from these slips will be shown as "unbillable" on reports.
Do Not Bill	For unbillable work that you do not want to retain after the billing cycle but did on behalf of the client.	Slip will not appear on a bill. Amounts from these slips will be shown as "unbillable" on reports. Slips will be marked "recorded" once bill for client and time period is finalized.
Summary	Used to group slips for a specific client and activity code on a bill. Summary slips must be created for each client and each activity for that client that you wish summarized.	Used primarily with expenses when want to summarize expenses by type with more text than permitted by using the Activity Summary option. Can be used for some activities and not others. Full name option in activity is a alternative available only in Version 7.

CHAPTER TWO

Lesson 2: Entering Disbursements

OBJECTIVE: TO ENTER YOUR EXPENSES directly into Timeslips.

As with the lesson on entering your time, your first task is to get to the TSTimer window. Follow the instructions in Chapter 1 to get to the TSTimer screen.

1. If you have an existing slip displayed, you need to start a new slip. The fastest way to do this is to press **CTRL+N.** (If you really hate to use the keyboard, you can use your mouse to click on the **NEW** button on the right-hand side of the screen.) If you are already at a new slip, continue below.

    Once you have instructed Timeslips to start a new slip, you are ready to enter the information. The way the program knows that this is an expense slip rather than a time slip is through the use of a "$" at the beginning of expense-based activity codes. It is not necessary to click on the Expense slip button near the top left corner of the screen. As you can see in Figure 10, when you create an expense slip, the time-related fields change to Quantity and Price.

2. **Attorney (User) Nickname:** Timeslips requires a timekeeper's code to be attached to all expense slips. Most law firms are not concerned about *who* within the firm is associated with a specific expense slip. One simple solution to this requirement is to create an additional timekeeper, with the nickname "Disbursements." When you are entering expense slips, you simply select the timekeeper "Disbursements" for all costs. This technique will also assist you when you want to prepare reports. Rather than having to

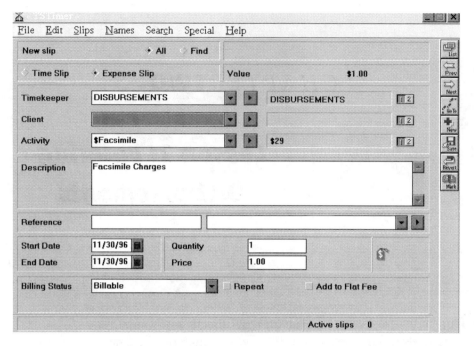

FIGURE 10. Expense Slip Entry Screen

mark specifically disbursement codes for a report, you can simply select to include any slips for the timekeeper "Disbursements." This also lets you exclude disbursements from any reports when you only want time-based information by excluding the timekeeper "Disbursements."

If your firm needs to track disbursements by the attorneys who actually incurred the expense on behalf of the client, you should enter the attorney's nickname the same way as you did for your time entries.

Type part or all of your attorney's nickname or start to type **D - I - S - B** until the timekeeper "Disbursements" is showing on the screen. As you begin to type, you will see the nickname you have selected. You can then press the **TAB** key to move to the next field.

If the nickname doesn't appear, you can look for it on the list of available nicknames by clicking the down triangle (▼) with your mouse or pressing **F4**. If your name is on that list, click on it to select it. Timeslips allows you to identify your timekeepers with two different nicknames. If the nicknames available from the list do not look familiar, try clicking on the number 1 or 2 button to the right of the nickname field to display the alternate set of nicknames. See Figure 5 on page 15.

>**Client Nickname:** Type part or all of the client's (or case) nickname until you see it appear in the field. If you have a lot of clients with similar nicknames, you may want to click the down triangle (▼) or press **F4** to pop up the list of available codes. Click on the client for whom you want to enter an expense and it will be inserted into the field. Use the **TAB** key to move to the next field or click in the next field with your mouse.

3. **Activity Code:** Type part or all of the Activity Code for the disbursement. Since you are now entering an expense slip, the Activity Code you will use must start with a dollar sign (**$**). If you already have expense codes entered in the program, typing a **$** in this field will bring up the first expense code on your list. However, in order for you to see how you can enter new codes on the fly as you need them, you will create a new expense code now.

Creating a New Expense Activity Code
You will set up the code for fax transmissions.

To create your new expense code, click on the triangle (▶) with the point facing to the right in the middle of the screen across from the Activity field.

>➤NOTE: If your firm has already entered its fax disbursement code, you can review its options by selecting the expense code you want to look at and then selecting Open instead of New after clicking on the right-pointing triangle.

Select **New Expense** if you are in Version 7 or later (**New** if you are in Version 5 or 6). This will bring up the Expense Activity Information Screen which is shown in Figure 11.

Nickname 1 and 2: You will see that Timeslips has already put the dollar sign into both nickname fields for you.

Type in **Facsimile** or **Fax** as Nickname 1, depending on how you like to refer to the code. (TIP: If you plan to use a bill format that includes Activity summary Expense style, this text will appear as the disbursement description for the particular cost.) You will notice that Timeslips automatically entered a number in Nickname 2. This is simply the next sequential activity code being entered and can be overridden if you want to use this field for an alternative code. If your firm uses code numbers, you can type in your own code as Nickname 2. If your firm is

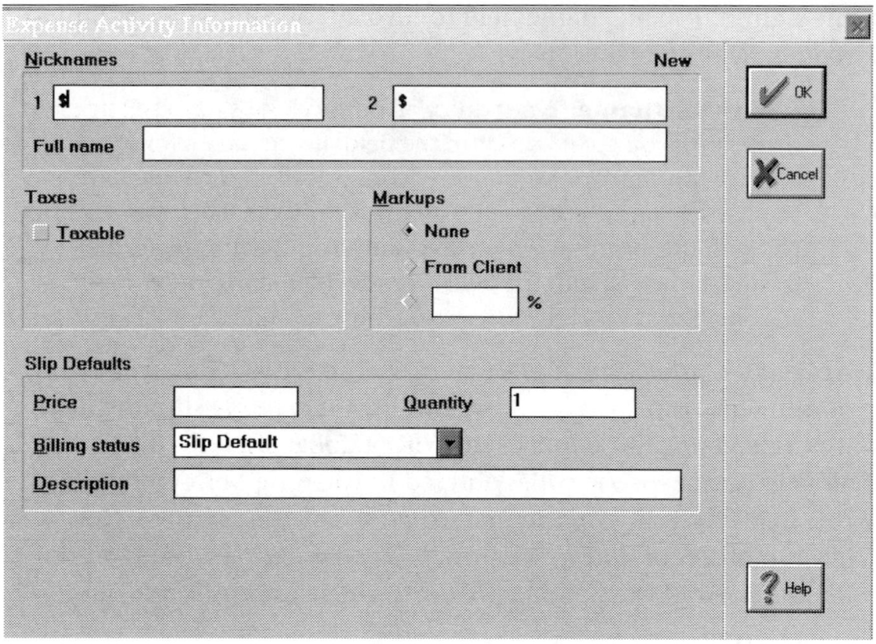

FIGURE 11. Expense Activity Information Screen

required to prepare task-based billing, you might want to put in the equivalent task code, which for fax charges is E104.

Full Name: This field is only available in Version 7 and above and was added for firms that are required to submit task-based billing to LegalGard, Lawtrac, and other legal-bill-auditing firms. In a task-based billing environment, the full name should be the task code followed by the task description. In our example, this would appear as **E104 Facsimile.** (NOTE: If you want this information to appear on your bill, you must check the Activity name box under Expenses on the Bill Format 1 view of each client's information screen.)

Taxable: In most jurisdictions in the country, lawyers do not have to charge sales tax for disbursements, so the Taxable box can be left unchecked.

Markup: For most firms and for most expenses, this should be marked **None.** The markup option lets you automatically add a defined percent increase to the actual amount entered as an expense. For example, in order to recover part of the monthly subscription cost for online legal research among your clients for whom you did research, you might charge a 2 percent markup above the cost of the actual search. If you have a global percentage, which you use for markups, check the From Client box for the activities you want to mark up and enter that percent amount in the Markup Slips by field on the Tax, Interest & Markup view of each client's information screen. This works best when the percent to be marked up is the same for all types of expenses. If, however, you want to define different percent markups for different expense types regardless of the client, use the third box and enter the actual percent to be used for this expense type.

Price: The Price field is used when an expense has a set price associated with it. This can either be a total price, such as with specific filing fees, or a unit price, such as with fax pages or photocopies.

Enter the price your firm charges per page for fax transmissions. You do not need to type the dollar sign or the decimal places if you are entering an even dollar amount (e.g., $1.00 would be entered as 1).

Quantity: Usually, the preset quantity will be one (1) for most types of disbursements. You would enter a specific number here only if your firm has a disbursement that typically has the same quantity each time. Otherwise, you will enter the actual number on the individual slips.

Billing Status: Unless you plan to give away your expenses, you should make your expense slips **Billable.** To do this, click on the down triangle (▼) and click on Billable.

Description: This field allows you to prerecord the text you want to associate with each disbursement. Here, you will enter **Fax Charges.** When you enter your slip, this phrase will automatically appear in the Description area. At that point, you could change it or add to it.

When you are done, your dialog box should look like Figure 12.

Click on the **OK** button on the right-hand side of the screen to save this code.

When you save your new code, it will automatically be selected along with the description you added, the billing status, quantity and price.

Use the **TAB** key or click in the Description area with your mouse to continue creating the slip.

4. **Description of Work:** The text you entered under Description when you defined this expense activity nickname will automatically appear in this field.

    If you used the **TAB** key to get here, the text will be highlighted. Be careful, since the next key you press could delete the highlighted text. If you accidentally delete text, you can try to undo (**CTRL+Z**) the deletion. Clicking the **Revert** button will undo the entire slip. Tab to the next field if you have no changes to make to this description. If you want to add more to the description, press the right arrow key (→) to clear the highlighting

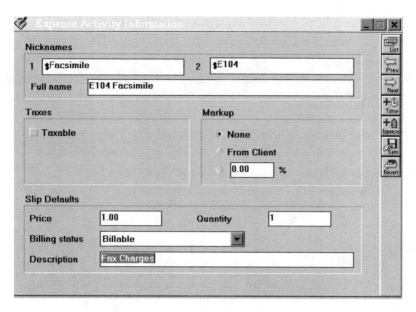

FIGURE 12. Completed Expense Activity Screen for Fax Charges

and leave you at the end of the description. Add any additional description you would like for this slip.

➤ *TIPS:* Most of the general Windows cursor movements and text-entry options work here. Use **HOME** to move the cursor to the left margin. Use **END** to move the cursor to the end of text near the right margin. You can also use **CTRL**+← or **CTRL**+→ to move the cursor from word to word. You can also use the mouse to highlight text you want to eliminate. Unlike your word processor, though, you cannot click and drag and do fancy editing here. Highlighted text can be deleted by typing replacement text, so be careful! In an emergency, **CTRL+Z** will undo a deletion.

Use the **TAB** key to move to the next field or click in the next field with your mouse.

5. **Reference:** The Reference field should be completed *Only* if your firm is using it for Matters, for task-based information, or for sorting purposes. If you are skipping the Reference field, use the **TAB** key to move to the **Start Date** field or click your mouse on the Start Date field.

To enter Matters directly, type an * (asterisk) before the Time-slips assigned matter number. If you are unsure which matter number to use, click on the down triangle (▼) or press F4 to search the list of existing matters, highlight the desired matter, and click on it to select it.

6. **Start Date** (**From Date** in earlier versions): Timeslips should already have today's date in the Start Date and End Date fields. If so, you can move directly to the Quantity field.

    If the date is wrong, you can type a correct one using the format ***mmddyy.*** There are a few neat shortcuts you can use to put the correct date into the slip. Take a look at "Entering Time" in Chapter 7.

7. **End Date** (**Thru Date** in earlier versions): Move the cursor to the End Date and type **S** to make it the same as the start date.

8. **Quantity:** If you are entering a fax disbursement, you should enter the number of pages of the transmission here. The quantity is the number of units to be multiplied by the price. If you are entering a different type of disbursement, such as a filing fee, you would leave one (1) as the quantity and put the actual price you want to charge in the Price field.

9. **Price:** When you defined the fax activity code, you set up the unit price for your fax charges. If you are entering a different type of disbursement, you should enter the price here. Remember that Timeslips will multiply the price times the quantity to determine the value of your expense slip.

10. **Billing Status Options:** Hopefully, all of your expenses will be Billable and charged to your client. If the options at the bottom appear to be correct, you are ready to save your slip. The other billing status options are explained on page 21.

11. **Saving Your Slip:** When you are done entering your information, you are ready to save your slip. Press **CTRL+S** or click on the **SAVE** button on the right-hand side of the screen.

    When you save the slip, Timeslips will attach a slip number to the slip and will show you the value (price times quantity) of the slip just above the timekeeper's name.

You are doing great!! You have now entered your first expense slip. If you want to start a new slip immediately, you can press the **NEW** button or press **CTRL+N** to start the new slip and save the one that was on your screen.

There are a few shortcuts you might like to know before you enter more slips. They are especially helpful when entering disbursements, since you are often entering a number of the same disbursement type at once.

CTRL+D	Duplicate Slip	Used to duplicate the *entire* slip. You can then edit the new slips for specific changes such as a different client or different price or quantity.
F8	Duplicate (Clone) Field	Used to duplicate the field from the previously displayed slip into the slip you are creating.
ALT+F8	Duplicate (Clone) Rest	Used to duplicate all fields from the previously displayed slips from your cursor location to the end of the slip.

Other Things You Might Want to Know about Entering Slips

In the lessons on entering time and disbursement slips, you have stuck to the basics. There are a number of other options here that you may want to know more about.

Editing Slips

There is no separate "Edit" function in Timeslips. If the slip you want to edit is displayed, you can make changes to it, assuming you have security clearance (through the program under **S**ETTINGS/Securit**y**/**1** User and your network) to do so. Remember to save the changes when you are done. The Revert button on the right-hand side of the slip entry screen will let you undo any changes before you save.

Go To

Select **S**LIPS/**G**o To or press **CTRL+G** to call up the Go To dialog box. In Versions 5 and 6, you can go to a specific slip number. This is helpful when you know the slip number and are editing slips at the end of the month.

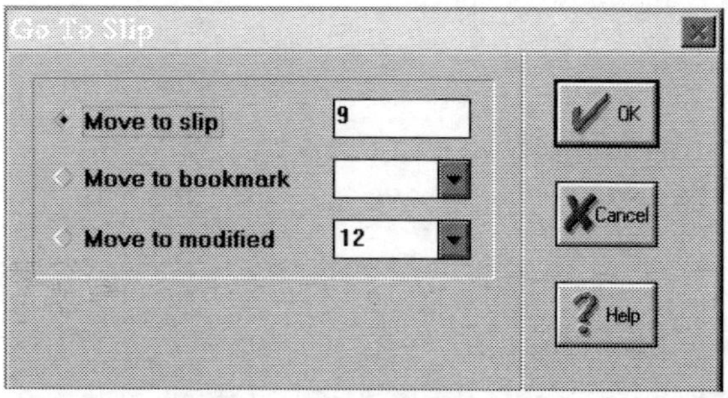

FIGURE 13. Go To Dialog Options

In Version 7 and 8, this function has been enhanced as shown in Figure 13.

In addition to being able to go to a slip by number, you can use the Go To option to move to a slip on which you have placed a bookmark or one of your recently edited slips. For the bookmark and modified slips, click on the down arrow (▼) and you will see an abbreviated list of the available slips. Click on the slip you want and click **OK.**

Search

Search provides you with several options. "Active" slips are those that have the timer on. Use the All Active, Active by User, or Previously Active to find your slips with their timers on or recently on. Selecting SEARCH/Criteria or **CTRL+F** allows you to select which information in which fields you want to be used to find slips within your Resident database file. For example, you could search for slips where you are the timekeeper, ABC is the client, and the slips you are looking for were dated between January 1 and January 31. You can even search for text within the description of the slip. You can also search for slips that have a certain bill status. Versions 7 and 8 add the ability to search for slips with bookmarks or limit a search to time or expense slips only.

Summary

Press **ALT+F9** or select **S**LIPS/S**p**ecial/Su**m**mary to see a recap of the work you have recorded. The summary will show you the number of new, edited, and timed slips you have entered and the amount of time and dollars they represent. You have a Clear button on the right-hand side so that you can reset this when you want. You might find this useful at the end of the day to see how much time you have entered. Your staff may find it helpful as a double-check to ensure that they have entered all of the written entries on a time sheet or disbursement log.

Bookmark

This feature was added in Version 7. You can attach a bookmark to a slip when the slip is displayed by clicking on the Mark button on the right-hand side or pressing **ALT+M** or choosing **S**LIPS/Add a **B**ookmark. Once a slip has a bookmark associated with it, you can use the Go To command, described above, to jump quickly to your slips with bookmarks. If you are looking at your slips with the List option, you can change your List view to see only the bookmarked slips.

MiniView

The MiniView was added in Version 6. One of the major benefits of Windows is the ability to have more than one program running at a time. It's frustrating to switch from one program to another when you really want to see both on the screen at the same time. The MiniView shrinks the TSTimer screen down to its core components for time capture and can be displayed in a small area while another program is showing. To change to the MiniView from the TSTimer screen, select **SP**ECIAL/**S**witch to MiniView or press **CTRL+M** from the TIMER screen. You can turn the timer on and off while the MiniView is displayed. Version 7 adds the enhanced Go To function to the MiniView.

Figure 14 shows the MiniView displayed in the upper right-hand corner while a letter is being prepared in WordPerfect 7 for Windows.

To return to the TSTimer full screen, you can either double-click on the MiniView or press **CTRL+X** to Maximize the screen. If you select SPECIAL/**P**references/**C**ontrol Options view, you can request that Timeslips start in the MiniView.

Slip List

The Slip List was a major enhancement to Version 7. Instead of looking at your slips one at a time, the Slip List lets you look at a table of selected

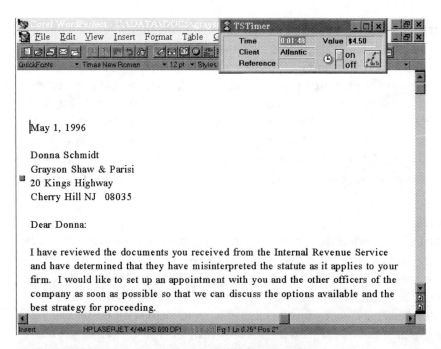

FIGURE 14. Miniview of TSTimer in a WordPerfect Document

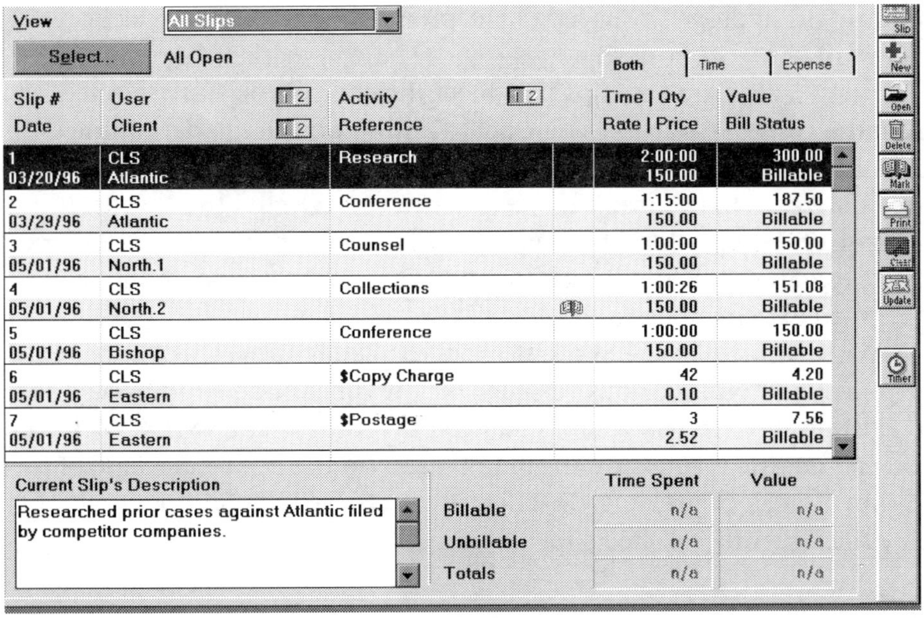

FIGURE 15. Slip List: List of All Slips by Slip Number

slips. Like the MiniView, it shows the critical fields from the slip. Figure 15 shows you the basic Slip List screen.

It consists of a View drop-down list, where you can select a subset of slips to review such as the recently modified slips or those that you have marked with a bookmark, a Select button that can be used to limit the displayed slips to a particular timekeeper or client or group of timekeepers or clients, and tabs in the upper right-hand corner to let you see both time and expense slips or only time or only expense slips.

Each slip shows the slip number, the Start Date for the slip, the timekeeper, client, activity, reference if entered, time and rate for time slips, quantity and price for expense slips, the amount of the slip, and its billing status. In the lower left-hand corner, you will find the description for the selected slip displayed. In the lower right-hand corner, you will see totals for time and amount for the displayed group of slips. Again, this can be extremely useful to see what work you have accomplished in a specific period of time.

When you select the Slip List, which you can do by pressing the List button on the right-hand side of the TSTimer screen or pressing **CTRL+L** or selecting **S**LIPS/**L**ist, it will display all slips. If you select a different set of criteria such as your Recently Modified Slips or choose specific components such as a date range or user under the Select screen, you will get a dialog box that prompts you to "Make your selections and then press this button." To improve the speed of the program, make all the selections you want before continuing. Pressing the button marked "Update List" will bring up to date the slips that meet the criteria you have selected from the current database. The Update button on the toolbar on the right-hand side of the screen will let you incorporate any new slips that were entered into the firm's database since you selected this screen. In the case of Recently Modified slips, it will display up to the last 100 modified slips. Since it is not limited to the work you have done today, this can be an extremely useful tool.

While you are in the Slip List view, you cannot directly edit the text of your slips. You can, however, turn on the timer or add additional time to existing slips. To edit a slip, you need to return to the TSTimer screen. You can do this by pressing the SLIP button on the right-hand side of the TSTimer screen or pressing **CTRL+L** or selecting **S**LIPS/**S**lip. This will display the currently selected slip.

Preferences

Preferences are available under the S**P**ECIAL pull-down menu in Versions 6 and 7. The Preferences screen consists of five view panels: (There are some differences between Versions 6 and 7. There are no changes in Version 8.)

➤**Keyboard Options:** In Version 6 and above, you can use the Keyboard options to modify the keystrokes you use to operate TSTimer. You can set specific hot keys to move from one field on the screen to another. The **F6** key is used throughout the program to jump from panel to panel or screen to screen. In TSTimer, for example, if you start on User, pressing **F6** will jump you directly to the Description area. Pressing it again moves you to Reference and so on. The Keyboard Options under Preferences allows you to change the order that you can jump. You can also set hot keys such as **ALT+D** to move directly to the Description area of the slip. In Version 7, setting the jumping order is more intuitive. In addition to defining where the **F6** key will move you, you can also define where the Tab key will take you. You can also tell Timeslips to skip panels that you don't use regularly such as Time Estimated or Reference.

Display Options   This screen lets you tell Timeslips how you would like TSTimer to appear when you start the program. You can tell it where you would like the main window to appear, whether you want to see the program logo first, if you want to see both nicknames on the screen, and which slip you want displayed when you start.

Control Options   You will use Control Options to let Timeslips know whether you prefer to start in the slip screen, the List View, the MiniView, or the view you last used.

Alternate File Paths   If you are using the Summary window to see a recap of what work you have done and are working on a network, you can fill in a file name and location here to have Timeslips keep a log of your work separately from the other timekeepers on the system.

Speller Options   This will only be available if you have installed the Speller add-on program. You can have Timeslips interactively warn you about typos and add your favorite client's names in a personal dictionary.

Slip Defaults   This is only available in Version 7 and above. Setting slip defaults can save you a lot of time when you are creating new slips. Here, you can have the program automatically copy the client code and reference, activity code, or dates from the previously displayed slip. No matter how you are using Timeslips, you will probably want to set the slip defaults to copy the dates from the previous slip. If you use "Time" as your main activity code, you can have it inserted automatically too, by checking the activity code box. If you tend to use the timer to record your work, you can have Timeslips automatically turn on the timer when you create a new slip.

Exiting TSTimer

If you are going to continue with the next lesson, you should return to TSReport. If you got to TSTimer through TSReport, you will be returned to TSReport when you exit TSTimer.

When you are ready to exit TSTimer, you should select FILE/**E**xit or press **ALT+F4**. If you are using Windows 3.X, you can double-click on the Control Bar (the little minus sign in the upper left-hand corner of the screen) to exit this window. If you are using Windows 95, you can click on the X in the upper right-hand corner to exit this window.

You can exit TSReport following the same options to exit TSTimer described above.

Where to Go from Here

If you are the person in your firm who has to know how to do everything in Timeslips, you should continue with the next lesson, Entering Payment Transactions. If you are going to enter your own time and want to become familiar with the billing cycle and reports that can be generated, you can skip the next chapter and move onto the Billing Cycle chapter.

CHAPTER THREE

Lesson 3: Entering Payment Transactions

OBJECTIVE: TO RECORD THE PAYMENTS you have received from clients into Timeslips so you can produce accurate bills and get a reliable accounts receivable report.

As with the previous lessons, your first task is to get to the main screen of TSReport, with the Navigator displayed, if you are not already there. If you have an icon in your Windows Program Manager for **TSReport,** you should double-click on it.

If you don't have an icon labeled TSReport, follow whatever steps your office has set up to get you into TSReport.

Payment

Timeslips includes Payments as one of the types of Transactions you can enter for clients. From the Navigator, there are several ways you can get to the Payments area of the program:

There is a New Payment button on both the Bill Cycle and Transactions panels of the Navigator.

Alternatively, if you choose the Browse Client Information button from either the Bill Cycle Panel or the Client Panel, you can use the "Will Open to" dialog box at the top of the screen to switch to Transactions. (See Figure 16.)

After you highlight a client's nickname, click on **Open.** This will bring you to the Transaction screen for that client.

If you select the Bill Cycle panel of the Navigator, you can also select Browse Payments. This will bring you to the Client list where you can highlight a client's nickname. Pressing the **Open** button will show you

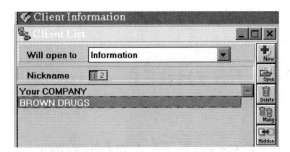

FIGURE 16. Browse Client Information: Will Open to Pull-Down Screen

the recent transactions for that client. Figure 17 shows a client's transaction screen. After you have learned how to enter a payment, we'll discuss the information on the Transactions List screen as well as how to deal with the other Transaction types.

If you start by Browsing Transactions, simply press the **NEW** button at the bottom of the screen to begin to enter a new payment. You will see a screen similar to Figure 18.

Type

Because you began by creating a payment, the Type is preselected as Payment so you can move to the Client box by either pressing the **TAB** key or clicking the client box with your mouse.

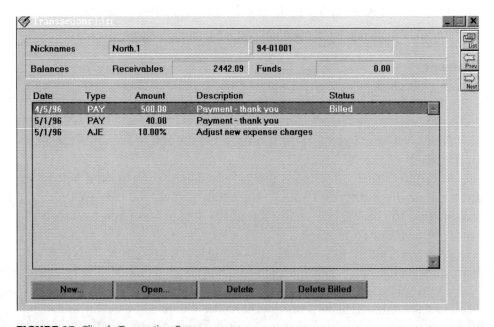

FIGURE 17. Client's Transaction Screen

Lesson 3: Entering Payment Transactions **39**

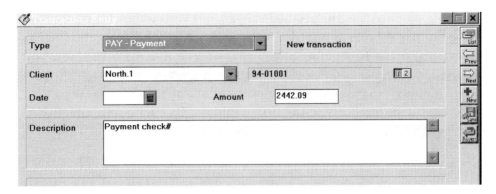

FIGURE 18. New Payment Entry Screen

Client

A client's name will already be displayed, but let us assume it is not the correct client. Type the first few letters or numbers of the nickname for the client whose check you want to enter. Remember that you can press the other button on the 1-2 box to switch to the other set of nicknames. If you prefer, you can press the down triangle (▼) or press **F4** to see the list of clients and highlight the client's name to select it.

Date

You can enter the date in the format ***mmddyy*** or type **T** for today. You can also use any of the date shortcuts described in Lesson 1. In Version 7 and above, you can use the pop-up calendar by clicking on the Calendar button next to the Date field or pressing **F9.**

Amount

This is where you enter the amount of the check you have received from your client. You do not have to type the dollar sign or the ".00" if the check is for an even amount. After entering the amount, press the **TAB** key or use your mouse to move to the Description area.

Timeslips Accounting Link: If you are using the Timeslips Accounting Link (TAL), you will have the option of attaching this payment to a specific invoice or applying it to previous invoices. You might want to purchase the link if you are using a general ledger program that is compatible with Timeslips. For most accounting programs, TAL is primarily a one-way link, that is, information from Timeslips can be transferred from Timeslips to the accounting program. Even if you are not using an accounting program that can link to Timeslips, you may find that some of the added capabilities of TAL or TAL Deluxe will provide you with additional information from the program. For example, it will allow you to associate payments with specific invoices and keep track of money received to pay off fees as opposed to expenses. Many lawyers (and their accountants) prefer to separate income from fees and costs. TAL allows you to divide payments and associate them with specific invoices. Additionally, TAL provides you with statements and reports that can be used to measure the profitability of the firm members, its clients, and practice areas. Contact Timeslips Corp. for additional information about TAL.

> ►WARNING: If you are using TAL, be sure to apply your payments carefully to the proper invoices. If you don't, you will end up with an incorrect accounts receivable report or inaccurate statements.

Description
This is preset to read "Payment - Thank you."

If you want to change the text that appears for this specific payment, highlight the text using your mouse or by holding down the shift key and pressing the arrow until it is all highlighted, then begin to type the new phrase.

If you want to change this phrase for all or even most payments, you can do this from the pull-down menus under **S**ETTINGS/**C**ustom Text/**T**ransaction Phrases. To change the Payment Phrase, type your new phrase in place of the one that shows next to the PAY - PAYMENT field and press **OK** when you are finished. This will not change the text for existing payments.

Save
When you are finished, you should save your transaction by clicking the **SAVE** button on the right-hand side of the screen or use the shortcut **CTRL+S.**

If you are done entering payments, you can press **CTRL+W** to close all of the open dialog boxes and return to the Navigator.

Adding More Payments
If you are fortunate to have more checks to enter, you can click on the **NEW** button on the right-hand side of the screen or press **CTRL+N** to begin a new transaction. Since it is also a payment, you can move directly to the Client field and select the appropriate client from the list. If the date is also the same, you can press **S** to keep the date the same, then move with your mouse to the amount field and enter the amount of the

check. Again, if the description is the same, you are ready to save this transaction and either enter another check or return to the Main Screen.

About the Browse Transaction Screen

When you want to review the payments you have received from a specific client, you can use the Browse Payments option to see recent activity. At the beginning of this chapter, we described the different ways you can get to the Transaction List screen for a specific client.

At the top of the screen, you will see both nicknames for the client you have selected. Just below this, you will see the client's current balance. If you are using the Client Funds option to store retainer, trust, or escrow funds during the duration of a case, you will also see the balance in the Client Funds account.

The center of the screen will show the date, transaction type, amount, description, and status of each transaction.

At the bottom of the screen, the **NEW** button lets you create a new transaction. The **OPEN** button will show the detail about the highlighted transaction. Use **OPEN** to edit a transaction before it has been billed and finalized. **Delete** lets you remove a highlighted transaction that has not yet been billed and **Delete Billed** can be used if you want to clear out all of the older, billed transactions from this client's record.

If you want to remove Billed Transactions from a large group of clients at once, you can do this using **F**ILE/**P**urge/**T**ransactions from the pull-down menus. Be sure you have a current backup of your database before you enter the Purge Transactions area of the program. Because it can permanently change your information, and because this book is intended as an introduction to Timeslips, you should follow the instructions in the Timeslips manual carefully before proceeding to remove billed transactions.

Other Transaction Types and When to Use Them

In addition to payments, Timeslips lets you change your client's balance or the amount he or she owes in the current billing cycle through different transaction types. A number of these are used in connection with

Client Funds. Client Funds are generally used for keeping retainer or escrow payments separate from general payments. See Chapter 6 on Special Handling: Flat Fees and Monthly Retainers for additional information.

To use these other transaction types, you will follow the basic steps outlined above for entering payments and then select the specific transaction type you want. Special considerations are noted below in the How to Use column.

The chart on pages 43-44 lists the Transaction type available and when and how to use them.

Lesson 3: Entering Payment Transactions 43

TRANSACTION TYPE	WHEN TO USE	COMMENTS
PAY - Payment	When you receive a payment from a client	Read this chapter!
CRE - Credit	Used to reduce a client's balance *after* the client has already been billed. Also used to write off an uncollectible balance. This reduces the previous balance.	Be sure to change the description so it is clear on the client's bill if the client is to receive the copy of the bill. You might use a phrase such as "Credit against previous balance as agreed in telephone discussion on such a date."
REF - Refund	Used when a client overpays the amount due. This amount is added to the client's prior balance to reverse the effects of the overpayment.	Do your clients *really* overpay?
PFA - Payment from account	This is used to reduce the balance in the Client Funds account for this client and reduces the amount owed by the client to the firm based on the client's outstanding receivables balance.	You may want to change the description to "Retainer applied to balance."
PTA - Payment to account	This is used to increase the amount in the Client Funds account for the client.	You may want to change the description to "Retainer received."
DTA - Deposit to account	This is used to increase the amount in the Client Funds account for the client. The difference between this and the PTA is that this is intended to be used when the source of the payment is someone other than your client and you want to track this separately.	You may want to change the description to "Retainer received from parent or outside party."

TRANSACTION TYPE	WHEN TO USE	COMMENTS
WFA - Withdrawal from account	This is used to reduce the balance in the Client Funds account for this client without affecting the accounts receivable balance. This would be used when you are using some of the client funds to pay third-party charges. This will reduce the balance in the Client Funds account.	You might want to change the description to describe the nature of the payment and to whom it is being paid. This is useful to distribute escrow funds.
AJT - Adjust time charges	This transaction affects only *current* time charges. This is typically used for deducting from or adding to a dollar amount on the current bill or providing the client with a percent discount.	You may want to change description to "10% Courtesy Discount." Be sure to check the Show box when reducing the amount the client owes so that it will show on the bill.
AJE - Adjust expense charges	Same as AJT but used to adjust expenses only.	See AJT
AJB - Adjust all charges	This transaction affects *current* total charges. Avoid using this option if you are using the Timeslips Accounting Link.	See AJT
FIN - Finance charge	Used to add a fixed amount to the bill. Usually a finance charge is automatically added through Client Information.	Rarely used in legal practices.
EXP - Expense	Alternative method for entering expense items on bills.	Left over from earlier versions of Timeslips. Do not use.

CHAPTER **FOUR**

The Billing Cycle

DURING EACH MONTH, you will set up new clients (hopefully, lots of them), enter payments (hopefully, lots of them too), and enter your time and billable expenses.

In many offices, the lawyer is not the person who generates the reports and the bills at the end of the month. Keeping this in mind, we have divided this chapter into two parts. The first part is an overview for the lawyers and staff to allow them to better understand the available options and recommended procedures for using Timeslips to prepare bills and manage their practice. The second part of this chapter is intended to assist the person in your office who actually does prepare the bills and reports. Even if you are not the person in your office preparing the bills, you may want to read the second half, focusing on the specific reports and steps you use in your own office. It is chock-full of tips and tricks.

Lawyers' Overview of the Billing Cycle

While more lawyers are entering their time directly into Timeslips, many still cling to written time sheets and have their time entered into the computer by staff people. Disbursements and payments are almost always entered by staff. At the end of the month, it always seems that there are pressing deadlines for work other than bills. In firms with several lawyers, reviewing billing work sheets can be a major bottleneck because the lawyer reviewing the work sheets also has to review the accuracy of the time entries of everyone who did work for that client, in addition to considering the overall bill. The better procedure is to have the individual lawyers proofread their time entries *before* the end of the month.

My solution to both of these problems is to create and run a **Daily Time Report** at regular intervals during the month. The instructions to create this report begin on page 56. The Daily Time Report is sorted by lawyer and then by date. This matches the order and format of a written time sheet and is easier for individual lawyers to use to compare their written time sheets with the work they did or to proof their work in that format if they entered their slips directly into the computer.

After printing the Daily Time Reports, each lawyer should review his or her entries to be sure there are no errors. The billing clerk can easily edit the slips since the report includes the slip number. You may wish to keep these edited reports as an audit trail of the work that was done, although the final versions will be incorporated on each client's billing work sheet. Otherwise, you can discard them once Billing Worksheets have been printed.

Depending on the volume of disbursements entered, you may want to have your billing clerk prepare and review a disbursement report just before the end of the billing cycle. This report would be similar to the Daily Time Report but would substitute Quantity and Price for Time Spent and add the Expense Activity codes. You might sort the **Disbursement Detail Report** by Expense (Activity Code) type and then by date to make it easier to see the expenses and compare them to the original records.

Before printing billing work sheets at the end of the month, I recommend that the billing clerk print a **Transaction Report** to verify that all of the clients' payments that have been received by the firm are entered and correct.

If any work is on hold, such as contingency work, estate administration or real estate transactions, you should review the **Charges on Hold Report.** This report will give you a summary of the amount of work you have held from billing. You can use this report to let your billing clerk know if you would like to see the details of any of these clients' work as a billing work sheet to determine if the client should now receive a bill.

Next, your billing person should print **Full Detail Pre-Bill Worksheets.** Billing Worksheets are referred to as draft bills or pro formas in other time and billing programs and as Pre-bill Worksheets in some of the versions of Timeslips. Once all the time, expenses, and payments have been entered for the billing period, you should print the Full Detail Worksheets and have them distributed to the appropriate lawyers for review and editing. The lawyers should consider the Billing Worksheet their last time to review the data to be billed to the client before the bills go out. If you use a limited number of bill formats and review your work regularly with Daily Time Reports during the month, you should be able to look at the Billing Worksheet and envision what the final bill will look like and be able to delegate the final proofreading and finalizing to your staff.

The Full Detail Billing Worksheets are the best snapshots of the work in process, payment activity, and prior billing activity for each case. Even if the final bill limits the information shown to the client, the work sheets include slip numbers, attorney initials, and rates. It is much better to edit the Billing Worksheets rather than the "draft" bill that lawyers often prefer. By including slips numbers, it is easier for your billing person to make corrections. Make sure that all of the data that needs to be in the system has already been entered. Set a regular date for billing and stick with it. The date range selected for your work sheets needs to be identical to the one you use for your bills to ensure you are seeing the same information your clients will see on their bill.

Beginning with version 6, you can use the **Billing Assistant** to edit your bills. The Billing Assistant provides you with a visual replica of your Billing Worksheet and allows you to click on an element and edit that part of the information. Figure 19 is an example of the Billing Assistant screen.

As you move your mouse pointer around the screen, it changes to a pencil when you pass over an area that can be edited. Clicking on that element brings you into the correct part of the program to change that information. For instance, if you need to correct a client's billing address, clicking in the name and address area will jump you into that client's

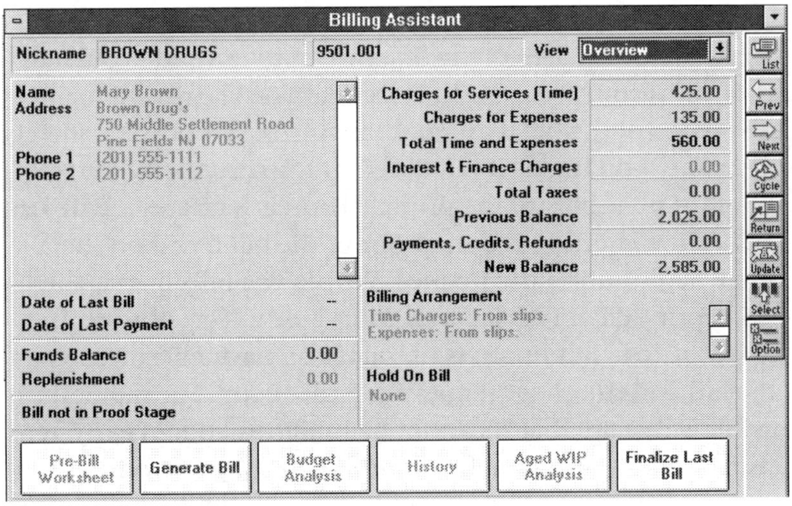

FIGURE 19. Client Information Displayed Using the Billing Assistant

Name and Address panel in the Client Information screen. The toolbar on the right-hand side will add choices for saving, updating, and returning to the Billing Assistant when you have completed your changes. Clicking the **Update** icon when you are back in Billing Assistant will bring the information up to date. The real benefit of the Billing Assistant is that you don't have to know which part of the program is used to make each type of correction to the client's bill.

Processing the **Bills** so they are finalized lets Timeslips know that the bills have actually been completed. Finalizing changes the selected slips from billable to billed. In fact, after billing, if you look at finalized slips in TSTimer, you will see an indicator in the upper right-hand corner that it has been billed as well as the invoice number it was on. In addition, finalizing records takes payments received and applies them against the clients' balances. Even though it seems like a waste, you should print bills with their final payments along with the months other bills so that you finalize the last payment. This will eliminate the balance owed by the client.

Before committing them to paper, you or your billing clerk should review the bills on the screen. Printing the bills to the display allows you to see them before you print them. At this point, you should be looking for formatting issues, such as whether or not you want a particular client's bill to show the rate charged next to each slip, as well as the overall accuracy of the bill. Make sure the bills include any adjustments and payments that should be credited on the bill along with any bill messages that should appear. Back up your database again if you have made any changes at this stage.

Although Timeslips includes several ways to undo or redo bills, ideally you want to make your bills perfect the first time through and avoid having to use any of the recovery methods. Depending on the reason for sending a new version of the bill, you might first see if it is possible merely to make an adjustment on the next bill to reflect the requested change.

When you print your bills to the printer, Timeslips creates a **Bill Image** of each bill. The Bill Image is a snapshot of the bill based on the printer you use when printing the invoice. Within the Bills menu, there is an option to Reprint Bills. This lets you print a new copy of the bill with its exact layout. The Bill Image is useful if you have misplaced your file copy of the bill and the client requests another copy. The major limitations of the Bill Image are that it cannot be modified and, in early versions of Timeslips Deluxe, it had to be reprinted on the same printer the bill was printed on. While you can also undo a finalized bill, you have a limited time period, namely until the next month's bill, when a particular bill can be undone. You would use Undo Finalization when you made a mistake on the most recent bill that cannot be rectified on the next bill. For example, you would need to undo a final bill if you calculated all of your time slips at the wrong rate and the client needs an accurate bill to submit for payment. If the client were satisfied with a correction on the next bill, you would use a Credit Transaction or Refund to offset the previous balance on the new bill. Alternatively, you could print a bill and choose to include billed items. This option does not include any previous balance information and requires you to recall the date range used in the earlier bill. Many law offices use the Include Billed Items option when they need to submit a fee petition to court or when a client requests a bill that includes all the work done to date on a single bill.

Even though you have three ways to reprint bills within Timeslips (Reprint Bill Image, Undo Finalization, and Printing Bill including Billed Slips), I find it helpful to add a fourth. After reviewing the bills on the screen display (after all, isn't this one of the reasons you wanted a network in your office?), I print the bills to a file. This file is in a generic format (ASCII) that can be opened in any current word processor. While I rarely use this file, it gives me two capabilities not directly available within Timeslips. First, I can edit a bill older than the previous month's bill to resubmit to a client. Be forewarned that the file version requires some formatting changes, particularly if you have used proportional fonts in your original bill. I would not use this option if the original bill does not include as much detail as your client now requests. The second benefit of printing the bills to file is that I can use these files to combine old bills together if a client requests a detailed recap of previous charges.

The importance of finalizing cannot be overemphasized. Processing your bills regularly gives you a more accurate financial picture of your practice.

As a bonus to the bills, Timeslips hides one of its best reports under the Options screen. By checking the box for the **Billing Worksheet Summary,** you get a report similar to Figure 20. While it has more information than most law firms need, it is one of the few reports that gives you the "big picture" for the month. It shows each client who had a bill printed, the invoice number, the billable and unbillable fees, costs and hours, adjustments, payments, prior balance, new charges, and new balance due. At the bottom of the report, it includes totals for the entire batch of bills. The totals are the numbers you should be monitoring each month to see if you are billing enough, have too much unbillable time or adjustments, what revenue came in, and how bad your receivables are. All in one report!

```
TSReport - [Billing Worksheet Summary]
File  Edit  Slips  Names  Bills  Reports  Settings  Window  Help

Account/                Billable      Unbill.                                    Prior bal
Last bill/              Fees/         Fees/         Tax on    Write up/   Payments/ New charge
Last charge/            Costs/        Costs/        Fees/     Write dn/   Credits/Pay+CR+Ref
Invoice #               Hours         Hours         Costs     Interest    Refunds   New bal

Atlantic                451.25        0             0         0           140.00    1162.00
  5/1/96                 54.50        0             0         0             0       1305.75
  10/7/97                 3.75        0                       800.00        0       -140.00
  10038                                                                             2327.75

Bishop                  125.00        0             0         0             0       1937.75
  5/1/96                   0          0             0         0             0        584.80
  5/1/96                  1.00        0                       459.80       144.75    144.75
  10039                                                                             2667.30

GRAND TOTAL             576.25        0             0         0           140.00    3099.75
                         54.50        0             0         0             0       1890.55
                          4.75        0                      1259.80       144.75      4.75
                                                                                    4995.05
```

FIGURE 20. Billing Worksheet Summary

After printing your bills to the printer, you are presented with a dialog screen (see Figure 31 on page 82) giving you the option to Finalize all bills, Finalize selected bills, or place them on **Proof Stage.**

Putting bills on Proof Stage flags them with their settings and options so that they can either be re-edited or finalized without having to be selected again. In older versions of Timeslips, operators had to cancel finalization of all of the bills being processed to correct a single bill. They also had to remember the exact settings and dates that were used to create the bills in order to match the information that was originally selected. Proof Stage is a halfway point between printing bills and finalizing them. If you put your bills on Proof Stage, you can clear individual bills from Proof Stage to make additional changes without disturbing the selection criteria associated with the other bills that were included in the same batch. If the bills on Proof Stage are satisfactory, you can finalize them directly from the Proof Stage screen without having to select or print them again.

If you are very careful in editing your bills, you can skip Proof Stage and Finalize all of your bills after they are printed. If you made a mistake, you can either undo the Finalization Backup and put your data back the way it was just before you finalized or you can undo an individual bill. For some people, the added step of Proof Stage causes more confusion. If you are one of these, edit your work carefully and simply finalize as you print the bills.

Version 8 added a new placeholder called the **Revision Stage.** Prior to Version 8, if a bill you placed on Proof Stage required additional editing, you had to clear it from Proof Stage. After making your corrections, you had to remember all of the settings (date range, etc.) you previously used. Revision Stage lets you push a bill back off Proof Stage for more changes while retaining the settings that generated it. To simplify editing a Revision Stage bill, the Version 8 Billing Assistant has tabs for included and excluded slips and transactions. If your settings were wrong, you still have the ability to clear the bill off Proof Stage and reselect your choices.

Getting More Information from Timeslips: Reports Overview

Depending on your firm's culture, your cash flow, and how you compensate the lawyers, you may want to produce reports after you complete your bills. Most firms print an **Accounts Receivable Report,** which provides you with a list of clients whose balances are outstanding. Beyond this, no two firms have identical needs when it comes to reports. You can try using the **Report Wizard** to select the information you want to see. If you choose to use the Wizard to create a report, be sure to note the choices you selected as you created the report so you can reproduce it later. The reports available within Timeslips are divided into eight areas: Slip Analysis, Worksheets, Bills, Client, Client WIP, User, Activity, and System Reports. Take a look at Appendix C for additional information about each of the available reports.

The **Slip Analysis Reports** focus on the information found in the time and expense slips. Many of these reports can be presented as either textual information or graphics in either bar graphs or pie charts. The User Defined Slip Report can be used to design your own reports. The Daily Time Report is an example of a detail-style User Defined Slip Report. The User Defined Slip reports can also be used to summarize slip information. For example, you might want to see a report that shows the total hours each lawyer has worked each day of the preceding month.

Billing Worksheets are a crucial part of Timeslips. The Full Detail Worksheet is your best source for seeing a snapshot of your client's work before generating a bill. The Totals Only version of the Worksheet is similar to the Billing Summary Worksheet in giving you an overview except that it focuses on unbilled work while the Billing Summary looks at billed information. The No Detail Worksheet gives you more information than the Totals Only but not as much as the Full Detail. It summarizes the fees, expenses, payments, and balances without the underlying detail.

Bills are the lifeblood of any billing program. These are your communication to your client to report the work you have done on his or her behalf and requesting payment.

Client Reports supply information drawn from the Client Information screens. Among the client reports are Name and Address Listing, Accounts Receivable Report, Transaction Listing (payments and adjustments), Monthly Totals, and a User Defined Client Report. The User Defined Client Report is similar to the User Defined Slip Report under Slip Analysis Reports except that it pulls together information from the Client Information screens.

The **Client WIP Reports** center on the work in process that has not yet been billed. These reports include several budget reports as well as the Charges on Hold Report. If you are charging Flat Fees, you may want to examine the Flat Fee Performance Report. The Aged Client Investment Report shows the work in process along with the accounts receivable balances for each client, allowing you to track how much you are owed by your clients. The Aged WIP shows unbilled slips in your defined aging periods to determine how old your unbilled work is.

The **User** or **Attorney Reports** compile data about the lawyers and other timekeepers in your firm. They provide information about rates, history, and other information taken from user information and history. Some of the User Reports include unbilled slip information to give you current information.

Activity Reports include an activity nickname listing that will show you your time and expense codes and their settings.

Buried under **System Reports** is the Abbreviations Report. If you have defined Abbreviations for shortening entry in time slips, this report will be an important reference. Under the System Reports menu are diagnostic reports for determining if there are problems with the database. There are also reports for printing out the list of custom client fields and global reference names, if your firm is using them.

Once you have determined which reports your firm wants to have produced, you should develop a checklist so that your billing person can run them regularly.

Billing Tips and Tricks

There are a few tips I have found useful over the years. You may find it helpful to print your Full Detail Billing Worksheets on colored paper so that they stand out on the lawyer's desk. In my office, we also clip the work sheets together so that I am forced to review all of the work sheets together and not separate some of them and delay getting the bills out. If there are one or two bills that I am not ready to send, I note that on the work sheets or request that the case be put onto hold. Some of my clients are given a red pen attached to the clip by their billing clerk to ensure that the edits made are easy to spot.

You should develop a coding system within your office to indicate what should be done with each work sheet. In creating your system, though, it is important to understand the terminology the way Timeslips uses it. For example, I indicate "DNS" on any bills that I want finalized but not sent to the client. The "Do Not Send" bills are usually ones where there is no new activity but a check has been received that reduces the client's balance to zero. This eliminates them from my Accounts Receivable Report since by including them in my billing, I am letting the program know that the final check has been received. Since I sometimes send bills with a zero balance to let the client know that the check has been received, I use "DNS" to indicate to my assistant which bills should not be sent. "Hold" has a very different impact than "Do Not Send." Slips or clients whose slips are On Hold do not get finalized. It is preferable to place a client on hold rather than hold individual slips. I mark work sheets with "Hold" when I do not want a bill prepared for that client. If a client has a previous balance, the Hold setting will not prevent the bill from printing. Timeslips will generate a bill with the previous balance and any new transactions (payments and adjustments). The bill, however, will not include new time or expense information because they are on hold.

I have never understood some of the convoluted filing systems I have seen devised by some law offices for storing the paper that is generated each month with Timeslips. It is much simpler to keep each month's information together instead of dividing everything up into a folder for each client. In most offices, it is the rare exception that requires a trip down memory lane to review old bills. Since you can get most of the historical information you need directly from Timeslips without consulting your paper records, why waste the extra time filing them for that rare occurrence?

There are many ways in which lawyers consciously or unconsciously sabotage a successful implementation of Timeslips. The two most prevalent are "focusing on the wrong details" and having "too many exceptions, not enough rules."

I am always amazed at the amount of time and effort lawyers will put into making their bill layouts just right. While I applaud the intent, often the inability of the program to incorporate one minor component gives the lawyer the excuse to criticize the entire program. One of my favorite examples was a lawyer who upon discovering, in an older version of the program, that we could not eliminate the underline after the disbursements, insisted his staff make the change on every bill in their word processor or with correction fluid. This lawyer lost track of the goals; namely, a timely produced, accurate bill with a clear enough format that clients pay with minimal questions or additional follows up.

While this phenomenon is not limited to the time and billing arena, lawyers have developed many techniques to "make work" for their employees in the billing process. Among the more noteworthy are lawyers who insist on individually printed envelopes instead of using window envelopes (when was the last time you didn't pay your credit card bill because you weren't impressed by the envelope?) or force staff to rework the bills to make minor changes. Remember that the goal of timekeeping and billing is to provide accurate bills to your clients on a timely basis. The bills should be clear so as to communicate services for which the client is paying.

The other major attempt to sabotage the system comes from having too many exceptions and no real rules. This most often happens in two ways: too many billing rates and arrangements or too many billing formats. While the legal market is more competitive now than it has ever been, there is no excuse for having more than a few different billing rates. If you have more than five rates for each timekeeper, you need to make a conscious effort to consolidate them or at least simplify them. While Timeslips can handle six rates per timekeeper, client rates and even complex rates based on your own rules (e.g., in-court vs. out-of-court rates), the more variations you have, the more vulnerable your firm is to making errors.

Ideally the firm should have one or two bill layouts. The layout is the structure of the bill and determines where the client's address will appear, what text if a Re: is entered and so on. The layout (TSLayout) is created in a utility that comes with Timeslips. The best situation would be a single layout, but for firms that need to comply with task-based billing requirements, a single layout may no longer be sufficient. Equally important, the number of the Bill Format options for your clients bills should be limited. The Bill Format, set on a client-by-client basis lets you decide whether to show dates, timekeeper, initials, hours, amounts, and so on. The Bill Formats are set in Browse Client Information. Even two or three formats with a modest client base can become difficult to monitor and maintain.

In my office, I have a single bill layout and two basic bill formats. The first format is used when there are multiple timekeepers working on the file. In this situation, I want my client to see who did how much work and at what billing rate. My other Bill Format is used when there is a single timekeeper working on the matter. Then, I do not need the same level of detail. Information about setting up the Bill Layout and assigning Bill Formats to specific clients is explained in Chapter 5, "Getting More Professional-Looking Bills."

Finally, remember that your billing program and its data is the financial lifeblood of your firm. Without bills, you will find it impossible to collect monies owed to the firm for work performed. Even if you have a tape backup system, I recommend doing an additional backup onto a floppy diskette as insurance. Many firms do not know how to restore information from their tape systems so having a floppy of your Timeslips data means that you can restore your data quickly and directly within Timeslips.

The rest of this chapter will focus on the gory details of the billing cycle. If you do not generate the bills for your firm, you should skim the rest of the chapter. If, however, it is your job to produce the bills, read on.

More Stuff about Reports

Each version of Timeslips includes more reports and options than its predecessor. While there are a few reports I consider critical to managing the billing process and keeping track of your firm's financial health, the type of information desired by different law firms is too varied to cover in this book. Timeslips, along with most computer companies, has shrunk its manuals and moved the information into On-Line Help. If you have access to the Internet, you may want to download the REPORTS.EXE file. This file expands into an Adobe Acrobat file that includes samples of all of the reports available in Timeslips.

Most of the reports in Timeslips based on information in the slips include Select, Sort, Template, Options, and Font screens. The other reports rely primarily on client information and historical billing information and usually do not allow you to specify date ranges to limit them. When creating slip-based reports, you can think of the **Select** screen as a sieve through which selected slips are permitted to pass. On the Select screen (which in earlier versions was called "Which Slips"), you can limit the selection to specific date ranges, lawyers, clients, activity codes, and custom client fields. On some reports, you can also use this screen to select slips by their billing status (e.g., billed, closed, or billable).

The **Sort** screen determines the order of the selected slips as well as any subtotaling options you want on those reports. The sorting can dramatically affect the appearance and value of the reports.

The **Template** for most reports is predetermined by Timeslips. The exceptions are the User Defined Slip Analysis Report, the Client User Defined Report, and, of course, the bill. These are very powerful tools that allow you to take information from Timeslips and put it in the format you would like. If these are not sufficient, your firm can purchase a report writer, Crystal Reports, a custom report designer that can create more complex reports. Every report in Timeslips can be printed to the screen (display), to the printer (based on your default printer in Windows), or to a file (often, in two different file formats: Report and Interchange). If you print to a file, the Report Format (in earlier versions known as Report Snapshot), creates an ASCII file that looks exactly like the printed report would look in Timeslips with the headers, footers, and spacing. It is a generic format that can be read by most word processors. In Versions 6 and higher, the Report format option lets you use tabs instead of spaces to separate columns. You should select this, if you have the choice, when you want to take information from Timeslips and change its appearance or order using your word processor. The Interchange Format creates a file commonly known as a comma separated, ASCII-delimited file—one that has the fields of information separated by quotes and commas. This file can be brought into a database or spreadsheet, or can even be used as a data file for merging in word processing documents.

The **Fonts** option allows you to change the fonts for any of the components of any report that Timeslips can produce, such as the Page Heading, Column Headings, Amount columns, and so on. Except for your bill layout, unless you have a problem with the predefined fonts, I recommend you leave them alone.

Daily Time Report

If the lawyers are entering their time directly into Timeslips, you should create and review a Daily Time Report to proofread your information *before* the end of the month when the bills need to be prepared. By checking the accuracy of your slips before the end of the month, you can avoid time crunches, limit the amount of time that billing partners spend reviewing associates' time, and possibly limit the number of people who need to review the billing work sheets during billing. Unfortunately, the Daily Time Report is not a built-in report. Although you could use the **R**EPORTS/**S**lip Analysis/**D**etail Listing, its layout is difficult to read and may include more information than necessary for your firm. Instead, I recommend creating this User Defined Slip Analysis Report, where you can select your own options.

To create and run this report, you can use the pull-down menus and select **R**EPORTS/**S**lip Analysis/**U**ser Defined. If you prefer using the Navigator, click on the Time and Expense Panel and select Custom Report. If you plan to run this report regularly, you might want to customize your Navigator and add a script with your basic settings selected. (This last option is beyond the scope of this book. Consider contacting Timeslips Corporation and hiring one of its certified consultants to assist you with customizing the program for your firm's specific needs.)

Template: The User Defined Slip Report Template should be set up to include the slip number (so you can go back and edit it), the client, matter (if you are using the Reference Number), description, and time spent. Some firms also include an amount column, although this distracts the lawyers from the proofreading task at hand. See Figure 21.

You do not have to include the slip date and lawyer since these will be your sorting options and they will show with subtotals. This will also help to make the report more readable. While I refer to it as the Daily Time Report, since it shows the description and hours for each timekeeper for each day, you can run this report on a weekly basis if it suits your practice better.

Start by typing the heading you want to appear across the report in the Title box at the bottom of the screen. The style for this report is Detail, so you can leave that alone. Detail style reports include a separate entry for each slip that is selected. Summary reports let you choose from fewer fields but are very useful for getting the "big picture" such as the total time each lawyer has worked during the previous month.

The **Field** section will let you choose which components of the slip you want to include. The **Format** options depend upon which field you

Date 10/29/97		Law Office Systems, Inc.		Page
Time 10:12 AM		Daily Time Report		
				Time
Slip #	Client	Description		Spent
Timekeeper - CLS				
345	BROWN DRUGS	Telephone call to client concerning status of litigation		0.40
356	HOFFER MOTORS	Review documents concerning pending litigation including defendant's answer and demand for bill of particulars.		3.50
387	SMITH GROCERY	Meeting with George Smith to discuss provisions for lease renewal.		4.00
Subtotal for Start Date 10/29/97				7.90

FIGURE 21. Daily Time Report

select. For example, if you choose Time Spent as your field, the format options will be in hours and minutes, hours, minutes, and seconds, or decimal. If you select Client as your field, the choices for format will be either Nickname 1 or Nickname 2.

Click on **NEW** in the middle of the screen. In the field labeled **Field,** you will need to scroll down until you see Slip Information. Highlight it and move over to the **Format** field. Select Slip Number by highlighting it from the pull-down list. Click on **Accept** to add this to our report. When you have entered the first field, your screen should look like Figure 22 below.

To enter the next field, select **NEW** again. In the field box, you want to select **Client.** This time, you may have to scroll up the list toward the top to find the Client field. Highlight it when you locate it, then click your mouse in the format box and select either Nickname 1 or Nickname 2, depending on how your firm is using them. Click on **Accept** to add this field to our report. If the lawyers in your firm want both nicknames on their report, you can use **NEW** again and add the other client nickname as the next field.

The last two fields I like to include are **Description** and **Time Spent.** They get entered the same way as the other fields. If you need to remove a field, highlight it and click the **Delete** button in the middle of the screen. The **NEW** button automatically adds the new field at the end

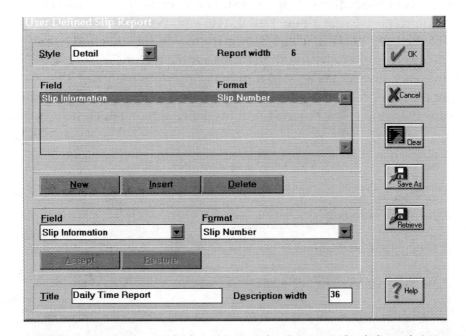

FIGURE 22. Slip Number Field Selected for Template for User Defined Slip Analysis Report

of the report. If you need to add a field in between existing fields, use the Insert button.

The **Save As** button on the right-hand side of the screen lets you save these settings so you can use the **Retrieve** button when you want to use them to run a report. You should press **Save As** when you finish selecting the fields you want for this report and assign it a meaningful name such as "Daily Time Report." Click on **OK** to leave this screen.

Select: Figure 23 shows a completed Select screen.

The **Select** screen should be set for the date range of the slips you want to review, the lawyer or lawyers whose information you want to include, and which activity codes you want included on the report. Depending on the version of Timeslips you are using, you have a number of ways to enter a date range. In all of the Windows versions, you can use **T** as a shortcut for today's date, **S** for same in the ending date field, type the full date in the format **mmddyy,** or simply type the number for the day you want if it is in the current month. These are the same options you have when you are entering time and expense slips. If you have Version 7 or higher, you can also use the Actual or Relative date options described on page 60.

You should exclude any disbursement activity codes (the ones that start with a $) if you have entered your disbursements under individual lawyers' nicknames. If you have entered all of your expense slips under

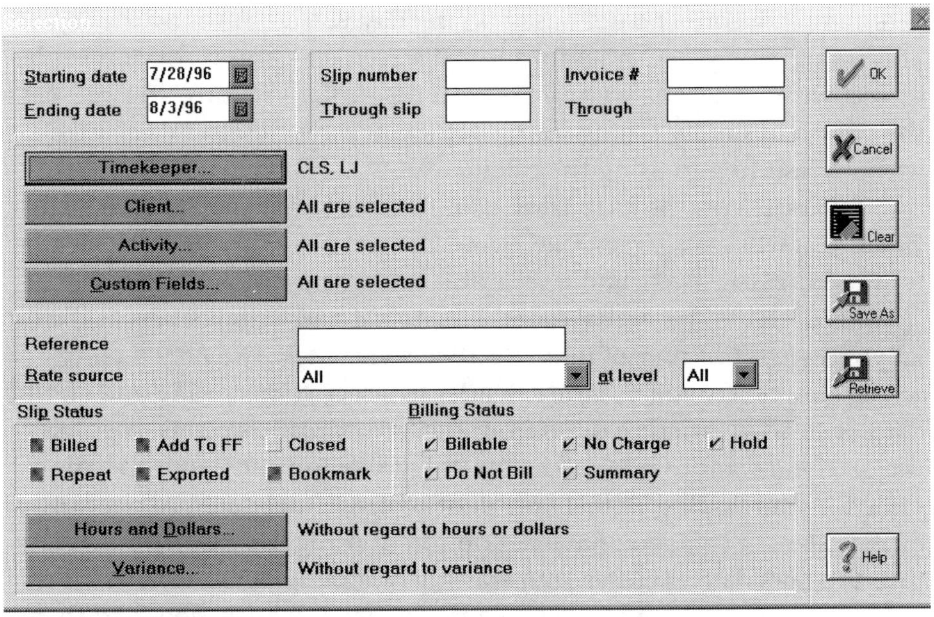

FIGURE 23. Selection Screen for Slip-Based Reports

the timekeeper "Disbursements" (as suggested on page 126) you can simply exclude that timekeeper from the list of lawyers to limit this report to time slips only. In the Slip Status area of the **Select** screen, you want to eliminate Billed Slips since the purpose of the Daily Time Report is to edit new work that has not yet been billed to your clients.

If you plan to run this report regularly, you may also want to save your settings in this screen the same way you saved the fields in the Template screen. In Versions 5 and 6, you should select all of your options except the dates. When you retrieve the saved screen, the only data you will have to enter is the date range you want to use. In Versions 7 and 8, you can incorporate the Relative or Absolute Date feature described below.

Relative and Absolute Dates

Version 7 added the option to select relative or actual dates and include them on your saved screen or in your macro scripts. Actual dates are those that never change. If you set an actual date for July 4th, it will remain July 4th. Relative dates change in connection to today's date. For example, if you want to run your Daily Time Report once a week, you can select a relative date range for the current week and have Timeslips determine the correct dates based on the day you are running the report. This means that you can set up a Saved screen *once* and it will forever be correct without any data entry. As with the earlier versions, you still have the option of simply typing in the dates you want to select or change without resorting to using the calendars.

If you click on the **calendar** icon to the right of the **Starting Date field**, you will see a screen like Figure 24. The screen includes a calendar for the **Starting Date** and a separate one for the **Ending Date.**

It is preset to use Actual dates. The Actual and Relative tabs at the top let you switch from Absolute to Relative style dates. The Actual date screen simply lets you use the calendar to select your starting and ending dates instead of entering them from the keyboard. To do this, highlight the date you want to use as your Starting Date and click on it. Do the same for your Ending Date if you want to use Actual dates. At the bottom of the calendar area, you have the option of using the **Today** button to insert today's date as either your starting or ending date.

When you click on the Relative tab, you will see a Period field that has a pull-down box. The two most common options for the Daily Time

The Billing Cycle **61**

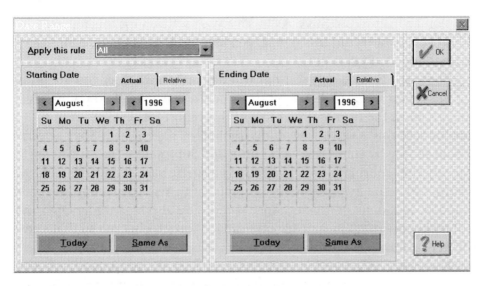

FIGURE 24. Date Range Screen for Selecting Dates

Report are Today or Week. If you select Week, you will see a screen like Figure 25.

In the Which Week field, you can select either this week (current) or the previous week (back). For the starting date, the Day in Period field should be set to First Day. At the bottom of the screen, you will be shown the date range that would be selected based on your criteria. After you set the Starting Date, you would move over to the Ending Date, click on Relative, select Week for the period and current or back for which week. For the ending date, you should use the Last Day for the Day in Period. Click on **OK** when you have made your date selection. Timeslips will insert actual dates in your **Select** screen, but if you have used Relative dates, they will change when you run this report later.

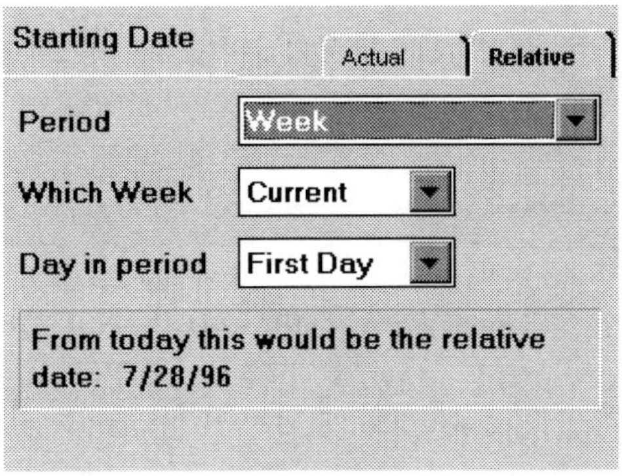

FIGURE 25. Calendar Using Relative Date Option

Don't forget to use **Save As** to save your settings for this report. When you want to run this report, you can use **Retrieve** to recall these settings and avoid data entry.

Sort: The **Sort** screen settings will depend on whether you are printing this report for a single lawyer or for several lawyers. If you only have one lawyer in the firm or prefer to run this report for one lawyer at a time by selecting a single lawyer on the **Select** screen, your **Sort** screen should simply be Start Date, Ascending and Subtotal by Day. If you are printing the report for several lawyers in a single pass, your first field for sorting should be Attorney with subtotals set to Yes. The second sort field would be start date. In this scenario, you should also look under **Options** and make sure that "Break Page on Primary Sort" is checked so that you will get each lawyer's time starting on a new page.

Review the other options there as well to see if any apply to you. For instance, if you use rounding (on the Client Information Screen, Tax, Interest & Markup view), you should check Apply Rounding from Client. You also have the option to Translate the Reference from the code (*#) to the description (e.g., Smith V. Jones) which was entered in the Client Information Screen under Reference (or whatever your label was changed to read). Finally, you have the option to double-space the report. This will make it easier to proofread but will use up more paper. The Show Selection setting allows you to see a summary at the top of the report of the settings you have selected to generate the report.

Options: The options that are available will depend on which report you are printing. The options for this report were described above.

Print: Every report in Timeslips can be printed to the screen (display), printer (based on your default printer in Windows), or a file (often, in two different file formats). You will want to print this report on paper so that the lawyers can review their time and make changes to any slips where the information is not right.

Figure 21 on page 57 shows part of a Daily Time Report using the settings described here.

Charges on Hold

If you keep any clients or slips on hold, you should run the **Charges on Hold Report** before printing work sheets or bills. The Charges on Hold report will give you an abbreviated look at the amount of time and disbursements on hold broken down by client. Under **R**EPORTS/**C**lient WIP Reports, is the option for the Charges on Hold Report. Even though

Timeslips gives you the option to refine the settings for this report, you should set the Select screen with no date range and all attorneys, clients, and activities. You do not have to worry about the Sort Screen settings for this report unless you want to sort the list by Billing Attorney.

> ➤NOTE: In order to do this, you need to have set up a Custom Client Field for Billing Attorney and selected the appropriate lawyer on the second panel of the Client Information screen for each client. See page 129 for additional information about setting up Custom Client Fields.

Lawyers in firms with a lot of contingency or estate cases, which remain on hold for an extended period, can use this report as a substitute for billing work sheets in that they can use it to review their inventory of work in progress without being bombarded with paper. In fact, in these circumstances, you might want to select a date range so that you can limit the report to only new work on hold during the last month.

Billing Worksheets

Billing Worksheets are referred to as draft bills or pro formas in other time and billing programs and sometimes as Pre-bill Worksheets in Timeslips. Once all the time, expenses, and payments have been entered for the billing period, you should print the Full Detail Worksheets and distribute them to the appropriate lawyers for review and editing.

If you have several lawyers in your firm, you may want to use a custom client field for Billing Attorney to choose to print the work sheets for the cases that lawyer needs to review. When printing the Billing Worksheets, choose the particular lawyer in the **Custom Client Field** part of the **Select** screen and change your **Sort** screen to sort first by **Billing Attorney.** To assist you in distributing the work sheets, you may want to print the custom client fields on each work sheet. Check off the Show Custom Fields box under **Options** to have the custom client field information print on the work sheets.

Figure 26 shows a sample Billing Worksheet.

The steps for printing the Full Detail Worksheets are similar to those described for the Daily Time Report, described earlier in this chapter. Select **B**ILLS/Pre-Bill **W**orksheets/**F**ull Detail Worksheet. Choose your date range and so on in the **Select** screen. Determine what sort you want, which options, then print. As you will see, Timeslips puts the date and time the report was printed across the top of the report. On the first page

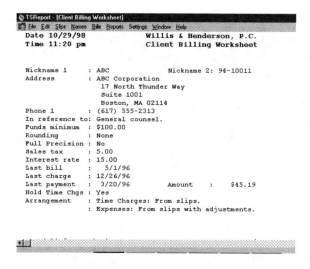

FIGURE 26.

of the Billing Worksheets, there will be a summary of the **Selection** settings. For each client or case, you will see the nickname and billing address, the last bill date, and the amount and date of last payment received. Below, it shows the detailed information from the slips including the slip number, so you can go back easily to edit anything on the slip, the date of the slip, the lawyer, activity code, description, number of hours, billing rate, and amount. If there is a flat fee or a time-based discount, this will appear after the time slips. After the time slips, it lists all of the expense slips with similar detail. It then shows the current balance, payments, and adjustments entered during the period, which will be applied on the bill, and finally the balance due. This work sheet includes client funds.

Select

The Custom Client Field option here can be used to work with groups of clients. For example, if you have defined a Custom Client Field for Billing Attorney, you can select All Attorneys in the large box on the screen (this will choose all the lawyers who have slips) and a particular Billing Attorney in the Custom Client Field (this will limit the report to those clients who have that particular Billing Attorney identified as the Billing Attorney on the Custom Client Field view of their Client Information screen). This will result in work sheets for all cases where the particular Billing Attorney has been entered on the second panel of the Client Information.

Another example might help you to understand the power of the Custom Client Fields. Suppose among your clients you have some who get billed monthly while others get billed quarterly. Rather than have to select them individually in the **Client** box on the **Select** screen, you can assign them a List Type Custom Client Field for Billing Cycle. Attach the appropriate billing cycle to each case on the second panel of their Client Information screen. On the Select screen, when you are ready to print your Billing Worksheets (or any other report for that matter), you can select ALL clients in the **Client** box and refine your selection further by selecting only the Quarterly clients in the Custom Client Field for Billing Cycle. (See page 128 for instructions about how to define Custom Client Fields and page 134 how to attach them to specific clients' records.) This technique is particularly useful for insurance defense firms who bill the insurance carrier on a quarterly basis, where the quarter is determined by when the case was opened. The trick here is to define three billing cycles:

Jan/Apr/July/Oct

Feb/May/Aug/Nov

Mar/June/Sept/Dec

When a new case is opened, assign the cycle that matches the month the case began on the Custom Client Fields view of Client Information. When you want to bill all cases due to be billed in July, choose "Jan/Apr/July/Oct" from the Custom Fields box on the report's Select screen. Not only is this self-maintaining in that you do not have to select each case individually, but you will not have to worry about omitting any cases that should be billed.

Depending on your needs, you might also create Custom Client Fields for semiannual cycles such as Jan/July, Feb/Aug and so on. For cases that get billed monthly, add a code "Monthly" and assign it to the appropriate cases. When selecting cases for reports, you would include Monthly, Jan/Apr/July/Oct, and Jan/July.

Sort

The Custom Client Fields can also be used in the **Sort** screen to divide up the Billing Worksheets by Billing Attorney. There are several different sort options you might consider, depending on your practice and personal preferences. The program comes with two predefined sorts: Bill Sort and Bill Sort by Reference.

Bill Sort simply sorts first by client and then by date. Bill Sort by Reference sorts by client, then Reference with a subtotal for each Case Reference, and then by date within each Case Reference. (Reference is one of the options for how to set up clients with their related matters. See page

92 for a discussion of using References. To use one of the predefined sorts, click on the **Sort** button, then click the **Retrieve** button on the right-hand side of the screen and select the sort you want to use.

If you prefer, you can create your own sort option. For example, I like to see my disbursements grouped by type with subtotals on my Billing Worksheets. I created a Sort by Activity, which sorts by Client with subtotals, by Activity with subtotals, and then by date. If you want to be able to sort your Billing Worksheets among the Billing Attorneys, set up Custom Field, Billing Attorney as your first field on the screen for this.

Font

Unless you have a problem with the fonts Timeslips has selected, you can skip the **Fonts** menu.

Template

Since this is a predefined report, there is nothing to do with the **Template** button.

Options

You should review the choices under **Options.** Among the options you might want to consider are to have your Billing Worksheets print the information in your Custom Client Fields, a timekeeper summary, your Bill Messages, or any private text you entered on slips or transactions. You can also have Timeslips check to see that you have entered the client's name and address (actually, it just checks for the first line of information) before it prints the work sheets.

Printing

When you have finished making your selections, click on **OK** and then select Output to Printer near the bottom of the screen and click on the **Printer** icon at the top right of this Window to print your Billing Worksheets.

Some lawyers prefer less paper to review at the end of the month and want, instead, to see the big picture of their current billing. If you prefer to review all of your time during the course of the month, you might want to run the Totals Only version of the Billing Worksheets to see the overview of your billing.

At this point, the Billing Attorneys should review the Billing Worksheets and make any corrections or changes. The advantage of working with Billing Worksheets is that they include the slip numbers and more information than the actual bills, making it easier for your staff to make the changes quickly.

Making Corrections with and without the Billing Assistant

The Billing Assistant is a dynamic summary of the upcoming client bill. It allows you to jump quickly to the source for the part of the bill that you want to change or correct. For example, if you want to change the client's mailing address, you can click on the address in the Billing Assistant, and the program will take you into the Client Information screen for that client, allow you to make the correction, save it, and return back to the Billing Assistant screen for additional edits. If you are using a version prior to Deluxe for Windows Version 6, you do not have the Billing Assistant. Even if you are using the Billing Assistant, it is important to know how and where to find the original information so that you can correct it properly and efficiently.

There are several common types of corrections you will want to know how to make using Timeslips. If you prefer not to use the Billing Assistant or have a version of Timeslips that does not include it, you can make the same kinds of corrections to your bills by accessing the part of the program that is the source of the information you want to correct. The instructions below, while geared to the Billing Assistant, can also be used to make corrections without the Billing Assistant. It simply takes a few more steps since you have to go to the parts of the program you want to change yourself instead of having the Billing Assistant take you there and back. The following table describes the type of correction and where to go in the program to correct it:

Type of Error or Correction	*Where to Correct*
Client Name or Address	Names/Client Info/Panel: Name and Address
Payment Missing or Incorrect amount	Names/Client Transactions
Slip Information (timekeeper, description, dates, amount or rate)	Slips/Make Slips
Hold Options	Names/Client Info/Panel: Flat Fee & Hold
Adjust Current Time	Names/Client Transactions/Adjust Time Charges
Adjust Current Expenses	Names/Client Transactions/Adjust Expense Charges
Adjust Current Balance	Names/Client Transactions/Adjust All Charges
Adjust Previous Balance	Names/Client Transactions/Credit

To use the Billing Assistant, select it from the Billing Cycle Navigator screen or under the BILLS pull-down menu. Highlight the client nickname for the case you want to begin correcting. When you select Billing Assistant for a specific client matter, you get a screen that looks like Figure 19 on page 47. At the top of the screen, you will see the two nicknames for the case you have selected along with the indication that you are on the Overview panel. The Assistant is divided into seven panels, which correspond to the information that comprises a bill. Instead of having to know what part of the program to use to edit the address, you can single-click on the address in the first panel and you will be able to edit the address as if you had selected the case from the Client Information screen and moved to the Name and Address panel. One of the benefits of the Billing Assistant is that after you have made a change, you have new options on the right-hand side that let you Update the information and Return to the Overview screen of the Billing Assistant for that case.

> ►TIP: While most of the changes you need to make can be accessed directly from this Billing Assistant, there are some, like the Bill Format screens, that cannot be edited directly from here by clicking on a displayed component. If you need to make changes to any of the Client Information screens, you can click on one of the fields in the first panel that contains the Name and Address information. This will bring you into the Name and Address panel view for that client's information screen. Click on the down triangle next to the View field near the top to switch to whichever view you want to edit. Save your changes using the **SAVE** button on the right-hand side of the screen and select **RETURN,** also on the right, to go back to the Overview screen of the Billing Assistant.

The Billing Assistant makes it easy to change information on time or expense slips. When your mouse changes to a magnifying glass icon, click on the time total or the expense total in the upper right-hand corner and you will see those slips in table format. Highlight the slip you want to edit and you will see the description associated with it in the lower portion of the screen. Double click on the slip and you will be brought into the TSTIMER or Make Slips portion of the program with the highlighted slip displayed on the screen. Make the edits you need to make. When you are finished, save your changes using the **SAVE** icon on the right-hand side of the screen or by pressing **CTRL+S.** Click on the **RETURN** button on the right-hand side to go back to the Billing Assistant. In order to see the changes reflected here, you need to click on the **UPDATE** button to bring the information up to date. Finally, the **RETURN** button will bring you back to the main screen of the Billing Assistant for this case.

If you need to change payment information or make adjustments to the previous balance the client owes, you should click on the Payments, Credits, and Refunds line in the upper right-hand panel of the Overview screen. This screen will then allow you to create a new Payment or Credit or edit an existing one. Again, before you leave the screen, save your work, select Return to go back to the Billing Assistant Overview screen and choose Update to incorporate your changes.

The Billing Arrangement Panel lets you make a number of changes to the client's bill. When the mouse pointer turns into a pencil on top of the words Time Charges, click and you will get a box with three options: Set Flat Fee, View Adjustments, or Cancel.

> Choosing Set Flat Fee will take you into the client's information screen that addresses Flat Fees. You will need to complete the type of flat fee (absolute, contingency, or percent complete are the most frequently used ones in law firms) and type any message you want to appear with the flat fee. If you are changing a client's billing arrangement to a flat fee, you may also want to change the bill format associated with the case so that you no longer show all the details associated with the slips. Before returning to the Billing Assistant screen, you should select the Bill Format 1 panel using the pull-down box next to the word View near the top of the screen. Review the settings here to show the information you want to appear on your bill. (For more information about the Bill Format screens, see page 135. For more information on setting up Flat Fees, see Special Handling: Flat Fees and Monthly Retainers beginning on page 105.) When you are satisfied with the options selected, choose **SAVE** on the right-hand side, then **RETURN** to go back to the Overview screen of the Billing Assistant, and **UPDATE** to incorporate the changes.

Choosing View Adjustments will allow you to either review or create any adjustments you are making to *current* work in process. You can access all three types of adjustments from this screen. New AJT is used to increase or decrease the fees or time portion of your bill; New AJE is used to adjust the expenses, and AJB is used to adjust the combined total of new fees and expenses. Note that these adjustments will not offset any prior balances. (Use the Payments, Credits Refunds field described above to adjust against a prior balance.)

If you want to give the client a 10 percent courtesy discount off the fees portion of the bill, you would select New AJT (Adjust Time). For the date, select the date that is the last day of your billing cycle to be sure this will be included with the slips you are adjusting. Be sure to change the description to something practical like "10% courtesy discount." For amount, you would enter **-10** and click on the percent icon. If you wanted to reduce the client's bill by a set dollar amount, you would enter a minus sign followed by the *difference* between the original amount and the new amount. For instance, if the original fees came to $412.00 and you wanted the client to be billed an even $400, you would enter a -12 as the amount. Also, check the Show adjustments on the invoice box to be sure your client will see your generosity.

You can also use this adjustment to increase the amount the client owes. You enter this the same way as you would the New AJT described above except that you would omit the minus sign since you are increasing the amount owed, you would enter a description for your internal records rather than for the client's eyes, and you would be sure that the Show adjustments on invoice is *not* selected so that the client doesn't see that you have written up their bill. As with flat-fee situations, you may also want to change the appearance of your bill so that you are not showing the hours worked, since they may no longer be accurate in light of the adjustment. You can use the Flat Fee option to get into your Client's information screen and switch to the Bill Format 1 screen and make the changes you need. Again, remember to save, return, and update.

The **SELECT** button on the right-hand side of the screen lets you limit the date range, slip numbers, or attorneys whose slips are included for all of your clients' bills. If you do not change this, Timeslips will automatically include all the slips and transactions that are currently in the system and have not yet been billed. Note that if you make changes to the Select screen through the Billing Assistant, you will be selecting those options for all of the clients whose information you want to view during this work session or until you change the Select screen option using another part of the program.

> ▶TIP: It's a good idea when you do access the Select screen that you check what information has already been selected. Use the **CLEAR** button on the right-hand side to start with all the information in the Timeslips database selected to be sure you start with a clean slate when you are preparing a new report.

The Hold on Bill panel gives you quick access to the Flat Fee and Hold panel of the selected Client's Information screen. Here, you can change the client to or from the different hold options.

Hold Full Bill will, unless the client has a previous balance due, put the case on hold and eliminate the case information from printing on billing work sheets and many other reports. This is helpful for estate cases, which can be active for an extended period of time but do not require regular review by the attorneys. In addition to Yes or No, you can also choose an amount option that lets you put a case on hold, without seeing report information until the amount to be billed reaches the selected threshold. Remember that if you put any cases on Full Bill Hold, you should routinely run the Charges on Hold Report. This report will summarize the billing information for clients who have any work on hold.

> ➤TIP: The down triangle associated with the Time Charges on Hold field gives you the choices of Yes, No, Amount, or Hours. Expense Charges are limited to Yes or No. Unlike Full Bill Hold, time or expense charges that are held with the Yes option will print on Billing Worksheets but will not be billed. The Amount option for Time Charges lets you put a case on hold until the amount specified has been reached through billable fees. Similarly, the Hours option can be used to put a client on hold until a minimum number of hours have been generated.

The Date of Last Bill and Date of Last Payment are merely there for informational purposes. They cannot be changed from within the Billing Assistant. The amounts in the Funds Balance and Replenishment can be changed here. These are described beginning on page 106. The panel in the lower left-hand corner of the screen is an informational screen that will advise you of the billing status of the case you are reviewing, such as whether it is on Proof Stage or not.

The **NEXT** and **PREVIOUS** buttons can be used to jump from one client's record to the next. If you need to work more selectively with your client list, you can use the LIST button to go back to the list and specifically select the client you want to work with.

The **OPTION** button is an advanced feature that enables you to decide which Navigator style buttons you would like at the bottom of the Billing Assistant screen. Making changes to this is unnecessary for most Timeslips users.

At the bottom of the Billing Assistant screen, you have the option of printing a Pre-Bill Worksheet, run a Budget Analysis, Client History, or Aged WIP Analysis, or Finalize the Last Bill. These are limited versions of the actual reports in that they will print only for the client whose information is displayed on the screen. The Pre-Bill Worksheet and Bill will give you the option to print the information to the screen display or to the printer. The other reports automatically show the information pertaining to the client who had been selected within the Billing Assistant.

Once you have made your corrections, you are ready to print your bills.

Backing up Your Data

Before you continue, you should be sure to back up your database. This is the optimal moment to do so since you have now corrected your raw information and are ready to process it. If you make a big mistake, you'll be thankful that you can restore from this backup and start over again. You should not rely on your firm's tape backup to handle this delicate procedure. Too many people in small firms do not have a clue how to restore from tapes or even to verify that the tape has in fact backed up the data. I would recommend regularly backing up the Timeslips database to floppy diskettes (one set for odd-numbered days and another for even numbered days) and to a file on your hard drive (change the preset name of TSBACKUP.BKU to something meaningful like 9709bil.bku, indicating the year and month, so that you know what this file is in the event you need to use it for billing cycle backups).

Timeslips also lets you back up your data without having to leave the program. Under **F**ILE/**B**ackup and Restore or on the File Maintenance panel of the Navigator is an option to **Backup** or **Restore.** If you regularly use Timeslips to do your backups, this first screen will give you status information about when and where you did your last backup through the program. Select **Backup** from the dialog box. It will then present you with a screen where you can specify the file name and its location. Use the Drives pull-down button to switch from your hard drive to a floppy (usually Drive A), use the Directories box to specify the location if you are storing the file in a subdirectory or subfolder somewhere on your hard drive, and use the file name field to change the name of the backup file. Once you press **OK,** Timeslips will create the backup of your database. Be sure to have a diskette ready if you are making your backup to a floppy diskette.

Printing Bills

Billing Overview

Timeslips, and billing programs generally, work best when you can process groups of bills together. Unless your clients insist on quarterly billing, you should aim to bill all clients at least once a month in order to improve your firm's cash flow. If you have a large number of open files, you may want to divide them up and bill half in the middle of the month and half at the end of the month. You can use the Custom Client Fields to divide your clients into two groups and choose the appropriate group on the Select screen. For this discussion, we will assume you are billing a group of clients at once.

The billing process itself has changed rather dramatically in the last few versions of Timeslips. Version 6 added a "Proof Stage." Version 8 added a "Revision Stage." You can think of Proof Stage as a temporary holding area for bills that are virtually ready to be finalized. It remembers the slips that were selected, date ranges, sorting options, etc. If a bill on Proof Stage is ready to send, it can be finalized without additional steps or it can be cleared from Proof Stage (Versions 6 and 7) or placed in Revision Stage (Version 8) to be redone. Prior to Version 8, if a bill you placed on Proof Stage required additional editing, you had to clear it from Proof Stage. After making your corrections, you had to remember all of the settings (date range, etc.) you had previously used. Revision Stage lets you push a bill back off Proof Stage for more changes while retaining the settings that generated it. To simply editing a Revision Stage Bill, the Version 8 Billing Assistant has tabs for included and excluded slips and transactions. If your settings were wrong, you still have the ability to clear the bill off Proof Stage and reselect your choices.

If your firm is conscientious about billing, you may find there is no need for either Proof Stage or Revision Stage. If this is the case, you can simply finalize your bills as you print them. The note below describes how to finalize bills without Proof Stage.

Finalizing is the process that moves all of the information forward in the program. It will change the selected slips from "billable" to "billed," create a balance due, age any prior balances, post any payments, apply any adjustments, and attach a Last Bill Date to the client's information screen. It is critical to finalize your work so that you can take advantage of having the computer track what your clients owe you instead of having to account for it manually.

> ➤NOTE: If you are using a version prior to Version 6, you can follow most of the steps associated with Version 7. Instead of putting your bills on Proof Stage, you should first print your bills to the Printer and not finalize. Make further corrections. Print individual bills as needed based on corrections. Ideally, you want to finalize your bills as closely after you print the client's copies as you can so that you can be sure that you select exactly the same clients, slips, and date ranges. Back up again if you have made additional changes. If you are unable to finalize immediately, be sure to check that you set the Revise Date (under Settings) back to the date when you printed the bills and review the options on the Select (or Which

Slips) screen for the same date range, same clients, and same Custom Client Fields. Also, be sure to use the same Sort Options and Options. If you don't have Proof Stage in your version, make sure no one adds or changes the amounts on any slips or transactions within the date range of your bills. This could cause problems in that the work sheets and possibly the client's bill might differ from the information finalized in Timeslips.

To finalize your bills, you will go through the same steps you did to print them the first time, including the Revise Date and Select screen options. When you get to the printing options, you should select File. This will give you a computer-based copy of your bills and eliminate the need to print the same bills again merely to finalize them. It's a good idea to create a BILLS subdirectory or folder within your file structure of your word processing documents to store these bill files since the files that are created are ASCII files that can be called up in any modern word processor and edited further. You should assign the bill file with a useful name such as 971125.BIL, where 97 indicates the year, 11 the month, and 25 the day within the month that was the ending date for the information contained on those bills. When asked, use the Default Settings and reply Yes to finalizing as well as doing the backup. (You can't have too many backup copies, and this one is particularly convenient if you need to undo the entire billing process.)

Revise Date

Unless you have turned it off under **S**ETTINGS/**P**references, each time you start Timeslips, it asks you to verify the date. What you are not told on that screen is that you can use this to change the date that will print at the top of your bill. In most firms, there is a delay between the cutoff date for slips and the date when the bills will actually be printed. If you prefer to have the date at the top of the bill match the date of the end of your billing cycle, use the Revise Date to set the date back. Additionally, you might print your bills one day and finalize them on another. In order to keep the date the same on the finalized versions and the client copies, change the Revise Date back to the same day you used when you printed the client bills.

You do not have to exit the program and restart to change the Revise Date. You can change this date inside Timeslips by selecting **S**ETTINGS/**R**evise Date. The date you choose here will be the one that prints at the *top* of your bill. This is totally separate from the date range of the slips that will be used to calculate your bill. The date range is done through the Select screen.

To print your bills, select **B**ILLS/**G**enerate Bills from the pull-down menu, press **CTRL+B** or click on the Generate Bills button in the Bill Cycle panel of the Navigator. (In some of the earlier versions of Timeslips, you need to select Bills and Reports, then Bills and Worksheets and then Bills to bring you to the same place.) Under Report Name, you will see that Bills has been selected. The Settings section has four buttons: Select, Sort, Options, and Template.

Select

Think of the Select screen as a funnel. Any selections you make on this screen limit the slips from the Timeslips database that will be included on your bills. Figure 27 shows the Select screen before any slips have been selected. If your screen shows some selections, click on CLEAR to reset the screen. Timeslips remembers settings from one report to another within a working session.

The Starting and Ending Date fields should be used to limit which slips are included on your bills. By including an Ending Date, you can have your lawyers and staff continue to enter new slips while bills are being prepared, although they should be warned about entering new "older" slips within the date range being billed. Be sure that you use the same dates for your bills as you did for your work sheets so that you

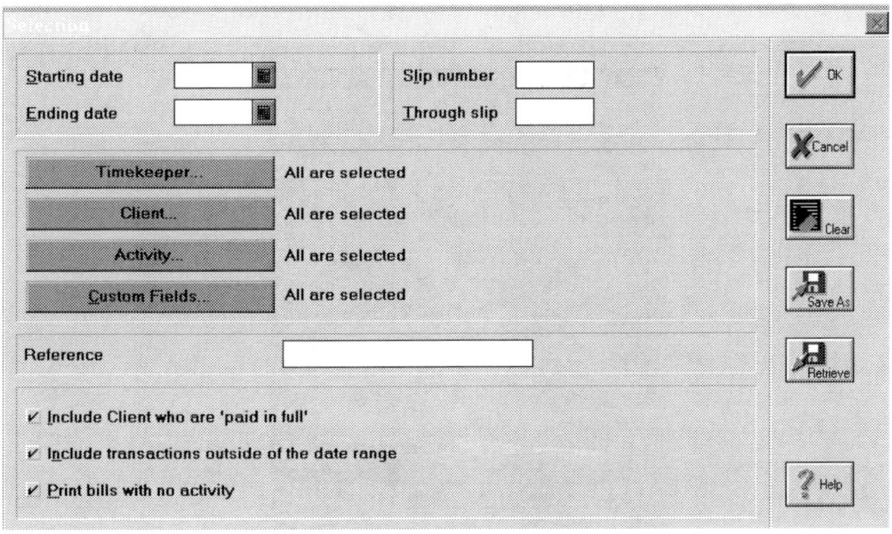

FIGURE 27. Select Screen with All Slips Selected (Default)

don't have any surprises. You can use any of the date entry shortcuts (described on pages 25 and 87) that are supported by your version of Timeslips, including the calendar icons available in Version 7 and above.

If you have a huge number of slips in your database, you might want to use the Slip Number and Thru Slip fields to limit the sorting of slips that Timeslips will do when it determines which slips to include on your bills.

Timekeeper

Generally, when you are preparing bills, you will want to select all of your timekeepers. The Select screen is preset to include all timekeepers.

Client

All clients are selected by default. If you want to print bills for all of your clients who have new work or current balances, you can jump ahead to the discussion about Activity Codes. If you need to select specific clients, you should click on the **Client** button. This will bring up a list of your clients with options to mark or select them across the bottom. See Figure 28.

If any clients have already been selected, in other words, it didn't say "All are selected" next to the **Client** button on the Select screen, you should click on the **None** button at the bottom of the Select Client screen to set them all back to No before selecting the ones you want for bills.

The quick way to select specific clients is to highlight any client code in the box, then type the first few letters or numbers of the client nickname you want to select. This should bring the highlight onto that nick-

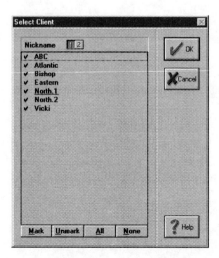

FIGURE 28.

name. You can either double-click with the mouse to mark this client or click on the **Mark** button at the bottom of the screen. Once you have selected all of the clients you want to bill, click on **OK.**

Activity
As with timekeepers, you will usually want to include all of your time and expense codes on your bills. If not, follow the steps outlined for selecting clients to limit which activity codes are to be included on your bills.

Custom Fields
Custom Client Fields can be an extremely useful way to limit which cases are to be billed in a particular session. For example, if you have set up a Billing Attorney custom code, you could select one of the Billing Attorneys here along with all clients and Timeslips will look at the custom field on each Client's information screen to select only those clients who are associated with the selected Billing Attorney. Similarly, if you want to bill only some clients on a monthly basis, you could use a Custom Client Field for Billing Cycle and select all the clients with that cycle in this screen rather than having to identify them individually in the Client selection screen. (Custom Client Fields are created in **S**ETTINGS/**C**ustom Client Fields and attached to individual client records on the second panel of Client Information. They are discussed in further detail on page 128. Custom Client Fields can also be used in combination. You could, for example, limit all clients by selecting a specific Billing Attorney and Billing Cycle.

Reference
You would only put information in this field if you want to bill a specific client and a specific reference. You may recall that Reference is one of the ways Timeslips can handle matters for clients.

Options
I recommend that you include bills for clients who are "Paid in Full," so that you can finalize the last payment along with your month's bills. (You may want to consider sending this final bill to clients along with a letter thanking them for their business and asking that they remember your firm when they, or their friends, need legal services in the future.) I prefer to exclude "transactions outside the date range" because I don't want to include client payments received after my billing cutoff date. If the payment is a significant one and I want to let the client know I received it even though it is not reflected on the bill, I include a note with

the bill either as a specific client bill message (set up on the last panel of the Client's information screen) or as a separate handwritten note. Finally, I like to "print bills with no activity." Bills with no activity are essentially statements since they remind the client that there is a balance due. If you have the Timeslips Accounting Link, you have the additional option after billing to prepare more-traditional style statements with a list of open invoices. I find the bills with no activity are more than sufficient for most firms' needs and eliminate an extra step.

You will notice several buttons on the right-hand side of the screen. **CLEAR** is used to change all of the settings back on the screen to their original settings; in other words, selecting all slips. **SAVE AS** is used to store all of the settings on the screen with a meaningful name that can be recalled using the **RETRIEVE** button. There are **SAVE AS** and **RETRIEVE** buttons on all Select and Sort screens and these can be convenient to avoid having to reselect the same options month after month.

When you have made all of your selections on this screen, click on OK.

Sort:

The Sort screen is used to determine in what order the slips you have selected on the Select screen will print on the particular report, in this case, the bill. Timeslips comes with several predefined Sort screen selections. By pressing the Retrieve button on the right-hand side of the screen, you can select Bill Sort. For bills, most firms can use Bill Sort, which sorts first by Client and then by date. If you need to sort first by Billing Attorney and you have set up a Billing Attorney Custom Client Field, you can **Insert** that field as the first field for the sort and then use **Save As** to save these settings for future use. Click on OK when you have made your sort selections.

Options

Figure 29 shows the options available when printing bills.

This screen is shown with the preferences I recommend. I prefer to have the program check for missing addresses before my bills are printed. Review Proof Stage bills isn't applicable yet since you haven't printed your bills. It should be selected, however, to ensure that you review these bills before printing and to make sure there are no bills remaining on Proof Stage from the last billing cycle that should have been finalized.

As far as I am concerned, the Summary Worksheet is the single most useful report generated by Timeslips. In a single report, it includes the client nickname, invoice number, number of billable and unbillable

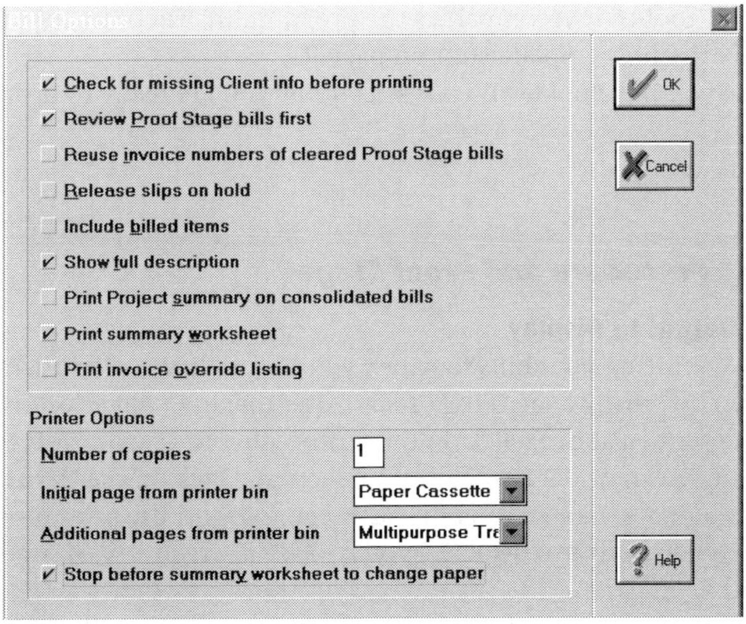

FIGURE 29. Bill Options

hours, number of billable and unbillable costs, and number of billable and unbillable fees. It also includes any payments and adjustments incorporated on the included bills. The totals at the bottom provide you with the big picture for the month, since they reflect the total dollars and hours being billed, the payments which were received, and the accounts receivable balance.

If your printer, as defined in Windows, has multiple paper bins, you can use the options at the bottom of the screen to have Timeslips pull the first page of bills from one bin and subsequent pages from another bin. Even if you don't have multiple bins, you could have first pages pulled from your manual paper feed. Of course, this assumes you haven't yet seen the wisdom of creating your own letterhead in the Bill Layout of Timeslips (a huge time-saver).

Template

Locate and select your firm's bill report template. If you haven't created your own or converted from an earlier version, it will be called DFLTBILL.RPT and is usually found in the main Timeslips directory, X:\TIMESLIP where X indicates the drive where your main Timeslips program has been installed. If you have a custom bill layout, it will have a file extension of .RPT. The template is prepared and customized in the

Bill Layout tool that accompanies the program. Instructions about how to modify the bill template start on page 91.

Once you have made all your selections, you are ready to print your bills.

Printing Procedure and Proof Stage

Review Output to Display

Before committing your bills to paper, you should first review them on the screen by printing them to Display. After making your selection settings as described above, click on the button next to Display near the bottom of the screen under the Output to: section. Click on the **Printer** icon in the upper right-hand corner of the screen to begin the print process.

When you "print to display," you will see a screen that is similar to Figure 30.

You will probably find it easier to review your bills on the screen if you switch from 100% magnification to 75% by clicking on the button in the lower left-hand corner of the screen.

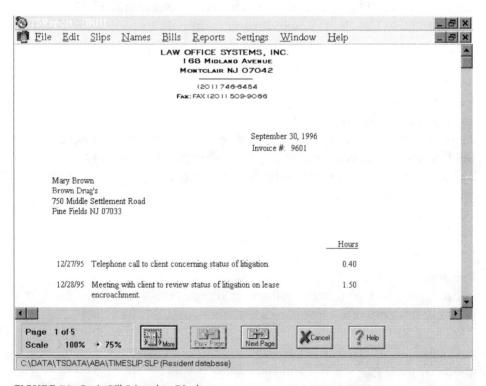

FIGURE 30. Basic Bill Printed to Display

The fastest way to examine the bills is to use the **More** button at the bottom of the screen. This will allow you to view your bills a screen at a time. If you need to go backwards, you can use either the previous page button if you want to move back to an earlier page or the vertical scroll bar along the right-hand side of the screen if you want to move up on the same page.

If you have properly reviewed your Billing Worksheets, you should not need to review the text and time elements of the bills on the screen. When you are reviewing your bills on the screen, you should be looking at the format to be sure it presents your information clearly to each client. For example, if the bill includes work done by several timekeepers, you should include the timekeepers' initials next to each slip. If they bill at different rates, you should include rates for each slip or use a User Summary Table to show the breakdown of work done by each timekeeper. When you reach the last page of the bills, the **Next Page** button will no longer be highlighted. At this point, you can click on **Cancel** to finish reviewing your bills on the display.

Make any changes to the bill formats in Browse Client Information and review the bills again on the display before printing on paper.

If you have not exited Timeslips and want to print the bills for exactly the same list of clients and slips that you just selected, you can do so without repeating all of the selection steps described above. Until you change your settings or exit from the program, Timeslips remembers the selections you made including the Revise Date. To print bills for the same group of clients quickly, press **CTRL + B** and go directly to the Output to: section of the screen and choose Printer. Click on the **Print** icon in the upper right-hand corner of the screen to begin the printing process.

Printing a Copy of Your Bill to a File

If you would like to have an ASCII version of your bills, you should print them to a File and then click the **CANCEL** button at the Generation of Bills Completed screen before reprinting them with the same settings to the Printer. The use of the ASCII version is described on page 49.

When you print the bills to a printer, you get the dialog box shown in Figure 31 on the screen after the bills have been printed.

Finalize Without Proof Stage

If you want to finalize your bills without putting them on Proof Stage, you can choose to either Finalize all bills just printed or Finalize selected bills from those just printed. The program will ask you to back up the database. The backup file will be called LASTBILL.BKU. It's a good idea to

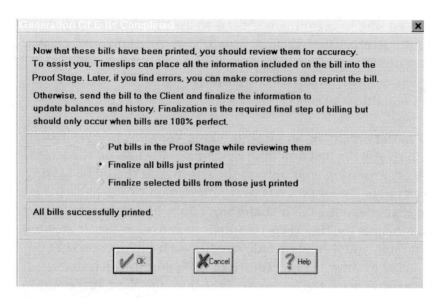

FIGURE 31. Dialog after Printing Bills to Printer or File

do this backup since it takes a snapshot of your data just before it actually finalizes your data. Remember, finalizing marks all of the included slips (billable and do not bill) as billed as well as payments and any adjustments in the selected time frame. Essentially, finalizing lets Timeslips know that the bills are ready to be sent to the clients.

If you want to use Proof Stage, follow the instructions below.

Proof Stage

One of the biggest problems in preparing bills in many law firms is the necessary delay between printing the bills for the lawyers' final review and actually sending them by mail to the clients. While you could finalize your bills at the same time you print them, most lawyers want extra time to look over the bills one last time before they are sent out to clients. As a result, you will not want to finalize the first time you print the bills on paper.

Finalizing bills is important in that it marks the selected slips as billed, creates an accounts receivable balance, and applies any payments and adjustments to current and previous work. Before Timeslips Corporation added the Proof Stage, firms had to be extremely careful in reprinting all of the bills in the same order, with the same revised date, clients, slip date range, and so on. The danger inherent in this procedure was that any discrepancy between the client's bill and the system's version could cause headaches. For instance, if more time for work before the billing cutoff date was added after the client's copy was printed but before the bills were finalized, you would end up with Timeslips thinking the client owed more money than he or she did and you would not have had that slip ready to be billed the next month. The Proof Stage is an elegant solution to handling the delay in printing and finalizing bills. Even though it is called "Proof Stage," you can really think of it as a proof list. Essentially, by putting selected bills on Proof Stage, you are flagging them with all of the criteria and slips that had been selected when they were printed, including the invoice number that Timeslips assigned to the bill. Instead of having to reselect the clients and slips, and possibly making a mistake by including or omitting information that had been on the client's copy, you can request that Timeslips finalize the bills that are on Proof Stage.

Proof Stage has several other built-in benefits. First, when you select to put your bills on Proof Stage, Timeslips prepares a bill image file for each case. If a client asks for a new copy of a bill, you can reprint it from the bill image that was created when you told Timeslips to put your bills on Proof Stage. Second, you can selectively remove bills from Proof Stage if you need to make additional changes without having to reselect all of the bills. Additionally, it enables you to review the bills to be finalized in an on-screen list that summarizes the information.

Until you have an opportunity to review the bills, you should select the first option: "Put the bills on Proof Stage while reviewing them."

If it suits your working style, you could print batches of bills or individual bills during the month and place them all on Proof Stage. Each bill would have the bill date for the day within the month that you put that bill onto Proof Stage and printed the bill. You could then finalize bills for all of the Proof Stage bills once a month to keep processing time down. This would also make it easier to take an individual bill off Proof Stage during the month if it were necessary to make a correction.

If you are working with either version 6 or 7, you do not have the Revision Stage option that is described below. In order to revise a bill that is on Proof Stage, you need to clear it. From the Bills in Proof Stage screen under the **B**ills menu, you need to mark the bill or bills you want to take off Proof Stage, then click the **Clear** button. You will need to print the bill again either to the Printer or a file. Again, depending on your preferences, you can either put it back on Proof Stage or finalize it. Remember, you always have the opportunity right after billing to undo a finalized bill or restore the Last Bill backup if many or all of the bills need to be redone.

Revision Stage

New in Version 8, the Revision Stage lets you make additional changes to bills that have been placed on Proof Stage without losing the original selection criteria associated with the bill. The dialog box for Proof Stage in this version is called Bills in Proof/Revision Stage. You can also automatically switch a bill on Proof Stage to Revision Stage by editing it through the Billing Assistant. Within the Billing Assistant, you can see the slips and information that has been included and excluded. Included items are those that meet the original selection criteria while Excluded items may have been added since the bill was put on Proof Stage. You can change the selection criteria for bills in Revision Stage by clearing them from the Revision Stage and starting over with printing the particular bill.

Finalizing Bills

If you are happy with how your bills look, the information on them is accurate, and they are ready to be sent to your clients, you are ready to finalize the bills. If you have put your client bills on Proof Stage, you will be given the opportunity to mark any bills that have not yet been finalized and perform the finalization process on them.

The best way to finalize all of your clients' bills is to select the same group of clients for whom you printed bills. (Don't worry if you forget some, though, since you will be reminded the case is on Proof Stage before you can generate a new bill for the same case.) Remember that by putting them on Proof Stage, you already informed Timeslips about the date ranges of information you want to include.

If you put all of your bills to be finalized on Proof Stage, you can process them immediately by selecting the Finalize Bills button from the Bill Cycle Navigator or BILLS/Finalize Bills. You can also get to these bills through BILLS/Bills in Proof Stage, which includes a button in the lower left-hand corner that lets you get to the Finalize Bills screen. You can even get to this by attempting to print new bills for the same clients as long as you have checked the "Review Proof Stage bills first" button under Options.

We will work through the route from BILLS/Bills in Proof Stage, where you will see a screen similar to Figure 32.

You can use this screen for several different functions. You can mark invoices here and then clear them to take them off Proof Stage. This will

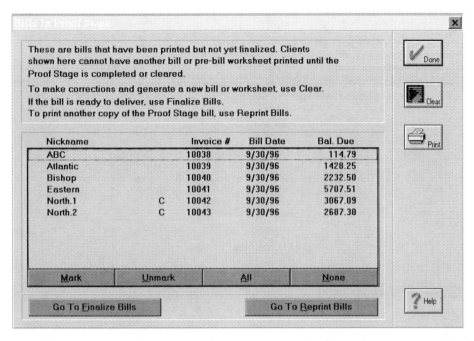

FIGURE 32. Display of Bills in Proof Stage

let you change the information in the bill before printing it again. To do this, highlight the bill you want to remove from Proof Stage by clicking on the Mark button at the bottom or double-clicking on the client's nickname. Marked invoices will have a check next to them. Press the **Clear** button on the right-hand side of the screen. Timeslips will ask you again if you want to remove the bill from Proof Stage. If this is your intention, reply Yes. If not, select **Cancel**.

You can select the **Go to Reprint Bills** button on the bottom of the screen to mark and reprint selected invoices. This will bring up a Reprint Bills dialog box. You can read more about how to Reprint Invoices at the end of this chapter.

You can also use this dialog box to process the bills you want to finalize. Don't bother to mark them on the Proof List screen since Timeslips won't remember your selection and you will be asked to mark them in the next dialog box. Once you press the Go to Finalize Bills button at the bottom of the screen, you will be able to mark those bills that you want to finalize. A sample of that screen is shown as Figure 33.

Timeslips will then ask if it is all right to create a backup. Since you can never have too many backups of your billing information, you should respond affirmatively. This backup will take a snapshot of the database *before* you finalize the selected bills. You can still undo a finalized bill without doing the backup, but if you want to put everything

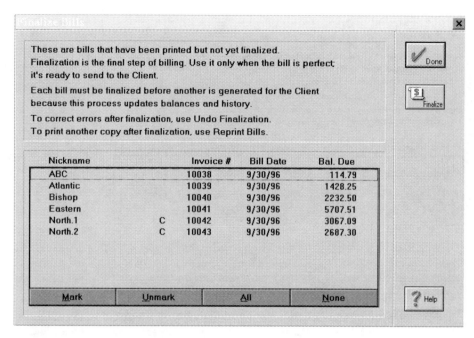

FIGURE 33. Finalize Bills Dialog Box

back the way it was, take the extra few minutes and do the backup. It is especially useful if you need to undo a bunch of bills.

Click on the Finalize button to actually perform the finalization process on the selected bills. When it is finished, Timeslips will let you know that it is complete and there are no more bills to be finalized. If you started this process by attempting to print the bills to a file, it will now ask you if you want to complete that process. Since it is really unnecessary, you can reply no.

You have now finalized your bills. This has marked all of the selected slips as billed with their invoice number and billed value, applied any payments and adjustments, aged any balances owed, and created a billing history that you can review when needed.

Undo Finalized Bills

Occasionally, things do not work out the way you planned. Even though you were careful in proofreading your bills, there are times when you simply need to undo a finalized bill. If you need to put the entire database back to the state it was in before you finalized your bills, you should restore the backup you made before you finalized the bills. If, however, you need to undo a single bill, the program allows you to select the invoice and undo a single bill. Select BILLS/Undo Finalization or from the Billing Cycle Navigator panel, select Undo Last Finalized Bill. Highlight the client whose bill you want to undo and then click on the **Undo** button. You can undo several bills if necessary.

If your bills are not available to be undone, it will say No in the Undoable column. If your bills are still on Proof Stage and have not yet been finalized, you will not be able to undo the bill since it hasn't yet been billed. There are several other circumstances that will make the Undo Final Bills unavailable. Some of these functions make the Undo function unavailable for all clients while some affect only the client associated with the operation performed. The chart below lists each of the functions that will prevent undoing bills and whether it affects all of the clients or the particular client.

Function	*Affects*
Purge slips, transactions, or TAL invoices	all clients
Delete slip or transaction	particular client(s)
Edit a billed slip (if allowed by security)	particular client(s)
Mass Update	particular client(s)
Deleting user or activity name codes	all clients
Edit client history or balances	particular client(s)
Clear client history from History Listing	particular client(s)
Edit or clear User History	all clients
Finalize TAL Transfer Register or Statement	particular client(s)

Reprinting Bills

Occasionally, a client requests an additional copy of an invoice. You go to your files and, for some bizarre reason, it is not there. What can you do? Version 7 added the capability to Reprint bills. The program can maintain up to 250 bill images per client including Proof Stage versions. Select BILLS/Reprint Bills or choose the Reprint Bills button from the Bill Cycle Navigator panel to bring up the Reprint Bills dialog box. You will see a screen similar to Figure 34.

You can highlight the client whose invoice you want to reprint. You will then see a list of available invoices. Mark the invoices you want to reprint and then press the **Print** button. If you have a large number of

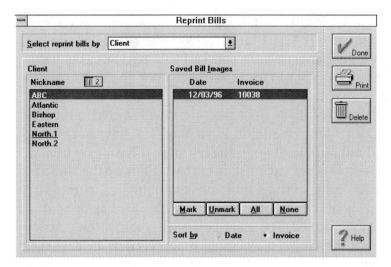

FIGURE 34. Reprint Bill Image Dialog Box

bills to reprint, you can also choose the **Criteria** button at the top of the screen. This will bring up a screen like Figure 35.

On the Criteria screen, you can select a group of invoices by date, invoice number, and client.

The two limitations of Reprinting invoices is that you cannot edit them and they must be printed on the same printer that was used to print the original bill. They are exact graphic copies of the original finalized bills.

If all other options fail (can't undo finalize and can't restore a backup) and you still need to reprint a bill and cannot undo a finalized

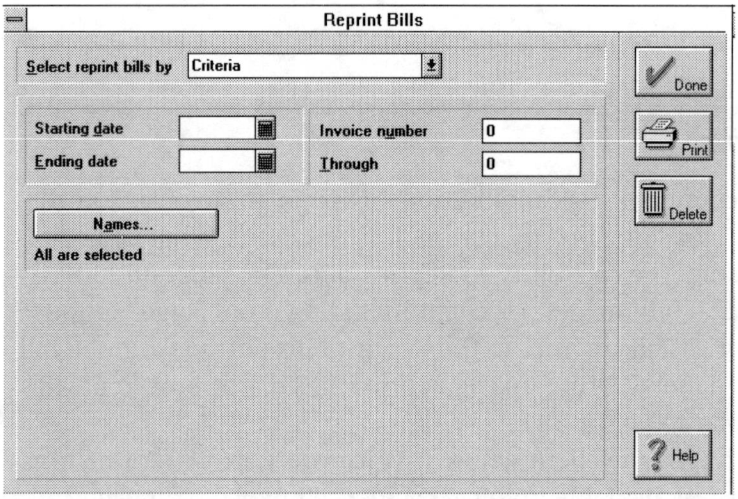

FIGURE 35. Reprint Bills: Criteria Selection Box

bill but need to change some of the information, you should proceed very carefully despite the desperate panic you are now in. Within System Preferences, you can get permission to edit billed slips. You should edit the slip information and then follow the normal steps to print a bill. When you are on the Bill Settings screen, choose options and check the box labeled Include Billed Items.

If your slips have been closed or archived, you need to recombine them into your Resident database. Be sure you have made a backup of your data before you do this as restoring the backup will be the easiest way to remove those slips from the database after you have rerun the bill with the billed slips included.

When you create a bill that includes billed slips, you cannot refinalize it. It will not include a balance or payments since they would not be accurate.

Conclusion

A lot of steps are described in this chapter concerning how to prepare bills. These steps are not difficult, but they do require a careful, step-by-step approach.

CHAPTER FIVE

Getting More Professional-Looking Bills

THERE ARE FOUR DIFFERENT PARTS of the Timeslips program that, together, determine how your client's bill will appear. They are the Bill Layout, the Bill Format screens in the Browse Client Information screens for each client, the Sort and Options screens within Generate Bills, and the actual time and expense slips. As with the other more technical parts of this book, we'll provide an overview first for those who want to understand the options and capabilities. This will be followed by more detailed instructions for those who need to implement the changes.

Bill Layout

The Bill Layout or TSLayout program is a special program inside Timeslips that is used to set up the *structure* of the bill and the phrases you want associated with your bill. The Bill Layout tool allows you to click and drag components of the bill such as the client's mailing address or the Invoice number to different locations on the page. Using the Bill Layout program, you can also change the order of the sections so that you can have an attorney summary table before your disbursements or move a general message from the bottom of the bill to the top. This tool also allows you to edit the phrases associated with the labels that print next to various amounts on the bill. For example, if you don't like the predefined "For Professional Services Rendered" as the description for the total fees due, you can change it here. Ideally, you want to have a single bill layout for all of the bills your firm produces. Sometimes, though, particularly when you have clients who require specific information on their bills, you may need multiple layouts. Ideally, you should try to use the Bill Format 1 and 2 views of Client Information to do as much of the client-level customization as possible. For example, suppose you need to send duplicate copies of a bill to the executors of an estate while only one is responsible for paying. Use the special message option on Bill Format 2 view to insert the cc's rather than adding another Bill Layout.

Bill Format

For each client or case with its own nickname, you have Client Information. The last two views of this screen (Bill Format 1 and Bill Format 2) control most of the bill format options that can be changed at the client or case level. The time and expense styles have the most profound effect on the bills. These options govern whether or not the text from each slip will print or whether and how the information will be summarized. Using the same basic information, we'll create four separate bills by changing the information on the Bill Format screens. Bill 1 on page 99 is a barebones bill with totals only for time and expenses. Bill 2 on pages 100–101 adds more detail. Bill 3 on pages 102–103 is a full-detail bill based on hourly charges and includes a bill sort by timekeeper. Bill 4 on page 104 is based on a flat fee. On the Bill Format 2 screen of Client Information, you can also decide whether or not to consolidate bills for multiple matters for a single client who has been designated as a key client. Timeslips gives you the choice of printing a separate bill for each matter, printing them on new pages in a single bill, or printing them consecutively on a single bill.

Sort and Option Screens

As you go through the steps required to print a bill, you are given the opportunity to make choices under each of the Settings buttons. The Select screen lets you determine which slips from the entire resident database will come through the funnel to be included on bills based on the criteria you select on that screen. The Sort option determines the order the selected slips should print on each of your bills. The Sort screen can also be used to change the format of the bill itself, particularly if you select to subtotal by one of the sort criteria. Among the ones commonly used by law firms are: Sort by Reference, Sort by Activity code, Sort by Attorney, and Sort by Custom Fields.

The Options screen includes a number of choices while printing your bills. While it is not recommended, you can, if necessary, select to "Include billed items," which will incorporate slips from already finalized bills. If you are consolidating bills for different cases for the same client, you may choose to select the Print Project summary on consolidated bills. This option creates a cover page that summarizes each of the matters included for that client. See Figure 36.

Time and Expense Slips

The final component to determine what a particular bill will look like are the raw slips themselves. How you describe the work you have done for your clients on your slips, how you have defined your activity codes, and whether you are using References will all help to define how your final bills will appear.

Changing Your Billing Layout

If you have never worked with any drawing tools, you may want to have a Timeslips Certified Consultant or a more advanced computer user assist you with designing your bill layout. Since most firms will generally

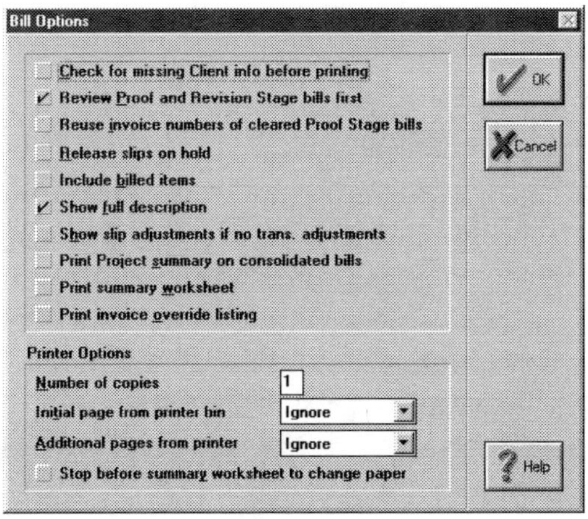

FIGURE 36.

have a single bill layout, it may be more cost-effective to hire someone to design your layout for your firm.

If you want to tackle this yourself, there are several concepts you want to understand. Before you mess up the Default Bill format (DFLTBILL.RPT) that comes with the program, you want to be sure to select Save As from the FILE pull-down menu in the Bill Layout program to save your efforts under a separate file name. You will be able to select it through the Template button on the Generate Bills Settings screen.

Figure 37 shows the Default Bill Layout in the Bill Layout program. To modify the components that you can see on the screen, such as your Company Name or Company Address, make sure the arrow in the upper left-hand corner of the tools is selected as shown in the diagram. Company Name represents the first line of Your Company's Client Information, usually your firm's name. Select it by clicking on the box that says "Company Name." It will then be lightly highlighted. In the lower left-hand corner of the screen, you will see its exact location. You can then drag it to a new location on the screen. For example, if you want to make the top of your bill look like letterhead, you might want to drag this up and to the center of the page. If you double-click on an item, you can set its size and location more precisely. In this instance, you might want to change the option to Centered on the page using the pull-down box at the top of the dialog screen. After pressing OK, you can make other

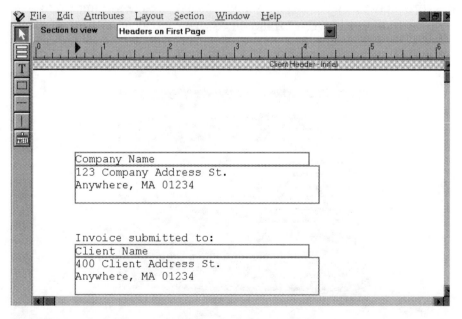

FIGURE 37. Default Bill Format in TSLayout (Filename: Dfltbill.rpt)

changes to this field. For example, you might want to switch the font from boring Courier 10 to one of the Windows true type fonts installed on your computer. To do this, while the field is selected, you can either choose **A**TTRIBUTES/**F**ont or press **CTRL+F.** This will give you a dialogue box that is similar to one you would see in your word processor or other Windows programs when you want to change the font of selected text. Notice that you can select a specific font and typesize, but you can choose a style such as italic, and designate that you want the text underlined. For Company Name, you might want to select an attractive font such as Times New Roman or Engravers Gothic, and set it on bold with a size of 14 point. When you return to the Bill Layout screen, you will see this field with the font and attributes you selected.

Some firms prefer to design their own computer-based letterhead instead of using the information from Your Company. To do this, you must first delete the Company Name and Company Address fields. Highlight one field at a time and press **DEL** to remove it. Most firms prefer to remove the "Invoice Submitted to:" field and you can do this by highlighting it and pressing **DEL** as well.

The "T," which is the third tool icon down on the left-hand side of the screen, is used to enter text directly onto the bill. Click on the **T** to depress it. Move your mouse to the approximate location on the bill where you want the text. Click and you will be presented with a dialog box where you can type the text. When you are finished, click on **OK.** Depending on the length of the text you typed, you may need to adjust the size of the box. You can double-click on the field to do precise sizing as well as positioning such as centered between the margins or, with text fields, you can click and drag on either of the small black boxes surrounding the text when it is selected to resize the box. As we did earlier, you can also change the font and attributes for this text. The "T" option is what you would use if you wanted to add the phrase "For Professional Services Rendered" underneath the client's mailing address.

The second icon down on the left side of the layout screen, which looks like three rectangles, is also useful in designing professional bills. By clicking on this icon and then clicking in the bill area of the screen, you will be given the choice of inserting information from a specific field on each client's information screen. For example, if you would prefer for your bills to include the phrase "For Professional Services Rendered from starting date to ending date," you can use the options here to combine a text field with database fields. Note that these dates correspond to the dates used on the Select screen, not the dates of the actual slips for each case. Perhaps that option will come with the next version of the program.

To edit a text phrase you have put into your bill, highlight the field, then select **A**TTRIBUTES/**F**ormat. This will let you change or correct any typos.

The box and line tools are used to add graphic lines to your bills. Most firms tend not to use these. The Paste jar is used to paste graphics into your bill layout. If you can put your firm's letterhead or a firm logo into a graphic format, you could use the Paste jar to insert it directly into the bill layout. The graphics must be either bitmapped (.BMP or .DIB) or Windows metafile (.WMF) formats to be pasted into Timeslips.

The other main parts of the bill that you may want to customize can be found under the **S**ECTION label of the pull-down menu.

Font Settings

When you select Font Settings, you will see a screen like Figure 38.

You can either change each component one at a time or you can select them all by clicking on the first item, then hold down the **SHIFT** key and press the down arrow until they are all highlighted. You can then select a different font such as Times New Roman instead of the Courier 10 that is preset on the Default Bill.

Phrases

The Section Phrases screen allows you to change the labels that Timeslips will use in connection with various sections of the bill. For example, I prefer to change "For Professional Services Rendered" to read "Total Fees Due" since it will appear on the same line as the total amount owed for the fees portion of each bill. The table below shows the phrases as they are originally defined and how I recommend changing them. I included only those that I recommend changing. You should review all of them to ensure you get the phrases you want.

Order and Attributes

SECTION/**O**rder and **A**ttributes lets you move the different sections of the bill around to change the order of presentation. The most common changes I have encountered are to move the flat-fee message above the time charges on flat-fee bills; move billing messages above the time

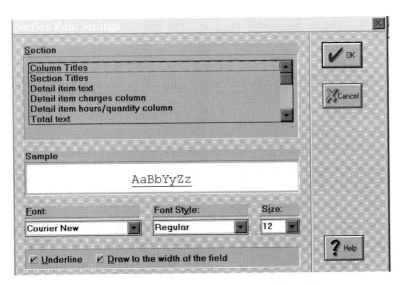

FIGURE 38. Use Font Settings to Change the Print on the Bills

Original Phrase	*Recommended Phrase*
Professional Services	(Make blank)
For Professional Services Rendered	Total Fees Due
Additional Charges:	Disbursements:
Total Costs	Total Disbursements Due
Total amount of this bill	Current Total Due
Previous balance of %CLIENT funds [NOTE: %CLIENT is a token that will insert the label you have used for your client nickname under Terminology, e.g. Client.Matter]	Previous Retainer Balance
Payments made from %CLIENT funds	Payments Applied from Retainer
Payments made into %CLIENT funds	Retainer Payments Received
New balance of %CLIENT funds	Retainer Balance
%USER Summary [NOTE: %USER is a token that will insert the label you have used for your timekeepers' nickname under Terminology, e.g. Attorney]	ATTORNEY SUMMARY
SUBTOTAL:	Matter Subtotal

charges on general bills; or to move the User Summary between the time and costs.

To move a section, highlight its description on the list, then press either the Move Up or Move Down option until it moves to the desired location on the list.

The Attributes option here controls indenting and spacing between sections. You can request Timeslips to start a specific section on a new page or not, add lines before or after a section, use lines around specific sections, or change the margins around a specific section.

Depending on how much you want to communicate to your clients on your bills, there are many more things you can do to customize your bills. Version 7 includes an option to create custom cover pages as well as reminder statements. These, however, are beyond the scope of this book.

Details for Producing Sample Bills

To produce each of the sample bills, the settings labeled below result in the different bill formats. Review them in order. Items that are common to subsequent bills are only indicated the first time they are selected. These samples represent some of the most frequently used formats for law firm bills. Most of the changes are made on the Bill Format 1 and Bill Format 2 views of the Client Information screen. You can also change the appearance on bills with more detail by changing the sorting options as you are preparing to print the actual bills. By changing the options on the Bill Format 1 and 2 views, you can make many permutations to change individual client's bills.

Bill 1: Simple Bill Format

LAW OFFICE SYSTEMS, INC.

168 Midland Avenue

Montclair, NJ 077042

(201) 746-6454 FAX: (201) 509-9066

Mary Brown   November 12, 1996

Brown Drug's

750 Middle Settlement Road

Pine Field NJ 07033

FOR PROFESSIONAL SERVICES RENDERED:

	Invoice # 9601
	Amount
[1] Total Fees Due	$1,290.00
[2] Total Disbursements	$65.00
Current Total Due	$1,355.00
[3] Previous Balance	$2,000.00
BALANCE DUE	$3,355.00

[1] Client Information/Bill Format 1 view: Time Style selected: Totals Only
[2] Client Information/Bill Format 1 view: Expense Style selected: Totals Only
[3] Client Information/Bill Format 2 view: Accounts Receivable: Balances

Bill 2: Limited Detail Format

LAW OFFICE SYSTEMS, INC.
168 Midland Avenue
Montclair, NJ 077042
(201) 746-6454 FAX: (201) 509-9066

Mary Brown November 12, 1996
Brown Drug's
750 Middle Settlement Road
Pine Field NJ 07033

FOR PROFESSIONAL SERVICES RENDERED:

[1] Invoice # 9601

[2] 10/15/96   [3] CLS   [4] Telephone call to client concerning status of litigation

10/17/96   CLS   Meeting with client to review status of litigation on lease encroachment

           LJ   Preparation of letter to client regarding actions required for completion as result of meeting with CLS

10/24/96   CLS   Meeting with client to review status of pending litigation

10/25/96   CLS   Review documents concerning pending litigation including defendant's answer and demand for bill of particulars

10/29/96   LJ   Prepare first draft of interrogatories for partner's review

10/31/96   LJ   Review and revise draft of notice of motion on upcoming appeal

           LJ   Revise interrogatories

11/1/96   CLS   Revise and review interrogatories

                                                          Amount

Total Fees Due $1,290.00

[5] Attorney Summary

Attorney	Hours	Rate	Amount
Carol L. Schlein, Esq., Partner	5.10	200.00	$1,020.00
Lee Jefferies, Legal Assistant	3.00	90.00	$270.00

DISBURSEMENTS

	Amount
Fax ⑥	15.00 ⑦
Filing Fees	50.00
Total Disbursements	$65.00
Current Total Due	$1,355.00
Previous balance	$2,000.00
BALANCE DUE	$3,355.00

① Client Information/Bill Format 1 view: Time style: Itemize
② Client Information/Bill Format 1 view: Time Charges: Dates
③ Client Information/Bill Format 1 view: Time Charges: Initials
④ Client Information/Bill Format 1 view: Time Description: All Paragraphs
⑤ Client Information/Bill Format 2 view: Timekeeper Summary Table
Rate: Hourly
Hours: Billable
Amount: Checked
⑥ Client Information/Bill Format 1 view: Expense style: Activity Summary
⑦ Client Information/Bill Format 1 view: Expenses: Charges

Bill 3: Full Detail Format

LAW OFFICE SYSTEMS, INC.
168 Midland Avenue
Montclair, NJ 077042
(201) 746-6454 FAX: (201) 509-9066

Mary Brown   November 12, 1996
Brown Drug's
750 Middle Settlement Road
Pine Field NJ 07033

FOR PROFESSIONAL SERVICES RENDERED:

			Invoice # 9601
			Hrs/Rate
10/15/96	CLS	Telephone call to client concerning status of litigation	0.40 [1] 200.00/hr [2]
10/17/96	CLS	Meeting with client to review status of litigation on lease encroachment	1.50 200.00/hr
	LJ	Preparation of letter to client regarding actions required for completion as result of meeting with CLS	0.50 90.00/hr
10/24/96	CLS	Meeting with client to review status of pending litigation	1.50 200.00/hr
10/25/96	CLS	Review documents concerning pending litigation including defendant's answer and demand for bill of particulars	0.70 200.00/hr
10/29/96	LJ	Prepare first draft of interrogatories for partner's review	1.50 90.00/hr
10/31/96	LJ	Review and revise draft of notice of motion on upcoming appeal	0.50 90.00/hr

	LJ	Revise interrogatories	0.50
			90.00/hr
11/1/96	CLS	Revise and review interrogatories	1.00
			200.00/hr

	Hours	Amount
Total Fees Due	8.10	$1,290.00

Attorney Summary

Attorney	Hours	Rate	Amount
Carol L. Schlein, Esq., Partner	5.10	200.00	$1,020.00
Lee Jefferies, Legal Assistant	3.00	90.00	$270.00

DISBURSEMENTS

11/3/96	Filing Fees for submission of notice to court [3]	50.00 [4]
	Fax charges	15.00
11/3/96	Fax charges	10.00
	Total Disbursements	$65.00
	Current Total Due	$1,355.00
	Previous balance	$2,000.00
	BALANCE DUE	$3,355.00

[1] Client Information/Bill Format 1 view: Time Charges: Hours
[2] Client Information/Bill Format 1 view: Time Charges: Rate
[3] Client Information/Bill Format 1 view: Expense Style: Itemize
[4] Client Information/Bill Format 1 view: Expenses: Charges

Bill Format 4: Flat Fee Format

**LAW OFFICE SYSTEMS, INC.
168 Midland Avenue
Montclair, NJ 077042**
(201) 746-6454 FAX: (201) 509-9066

Mary Brown   November 12, 1996
Brown Drug's
750 Middle Settlement Road
Pine Field NJ 07033

FOR PROFESSIONAL SERVICES RENDERED:

Invoice # 9601

[1] Flat fee message goes here. This could be a long message to describe the work that was done for the agreed upon flat fee.

	Amount
Total Fees Due	[2] $2,000.00
[3] DISBURSEMENTS	
Fax	15.00
Filing Fees	50.00
Total Disbursements	$65.00
Current Total Due	$2,065.00
BALANCE DUE	$2,065.00

[1] Client Information/Flat Fee & Hold view: Message on Bill
[2] Client Information/Flat Fee & Hold view:
   Type: Absolute
   Covers: Time Only
   Duration: Number of Bills = 1
[3] Client Information/Bill Format 1 view: Expense Style: Activity Summary

CHAPTER SIX

Special Handling: Flat Fees and Retainers

R*ETAINER* MEANS DIFFERENT THINGS TO DIFFERENT LAWYERS. While several other arrangements can now be handled by Timeslips, we will focus on the most common ones. Some lawyers consider a retainer an advanced payment to be applied against the first month's professional services. We will refer to this type of retainer as an "advanced retainer." To others, it represents the monthly flat amount paid by a corporate client regardless of the actual work performed ("flat retainer"). This type of retainer is often reconciled against actual time accrued at predetermined intervals. Sometimes, if you are lucky, you will have a flat monthly retainer ("flat fee") that is not compared with your actual work performed but represents instead the cost to the client of having you unavailable to their adversaries. Some firms treat their retainers like a security deposit and do not apply them to the conclusion of the matter ("deposit retainer"). Finally, some firms require a minimum balance in the retainer account during the case ("minimum retainer").

The good news is that every version of Timeslips since Version 3.4 can manage these types of retainers, although the earlier versions required more steps or slight work-arounds. Before deciding which method is right for your needs, you must consider the rules of professional responsibility in your jurisdiction and the specific language of your retainer agreement. Some states permit nonrefundable retainers as long as the details are clearly spelled out in your retainer agreement with your client.

Before we delve into the options of Client Funds, we should consider the simplest solution available. If your jurisdiction and retainer agreement allow you to request a nonrefundable retainer that will be exhausted in the first bill or two, you may want to treat it like a regular payment and change the description. Suppose you received a $2,000 retainer check from Ms. Brown to represent her in her unlawful dismissal from her job. To enter this transaction, we go into Client Information by clicking on the Browse Client Information button in Bill Cycle Panel of Navigator or pressing **CTRL+I**, highlighting her nickname. Above the list is a pull-down menu labeled "Will Open to." Click on the down triangle and select **Transactions**, then click the **Open** button. Once you are in the Transaction List Screen, click on **New**. The type is Payment and your client's nickname should be displayed. Enter the date the check was received and the amount as you would a regular payment. Change the Description to read: *Retainer Received*. (You might want to include the check number for your records. You can choose to suppress the check number from printing on the client's bill by preceding it with your private text character such as "!" which is established under Settings/Custom Text/Terminology). Then, click the save button or **CTRL+S** to save this entry. Review the steps for entering a payment starting on page 37 for additional information about Payment Transactions.

If you anticipate situations where the retainer payment is not exhausted on the first bill, you should consider entering a Credit Message such as *NO PAYMENT REQUIRED AT THIS TIME* under the Bill Messages option: Select **S**ETTINGS/**C**ustom Text/**B**ill Messages/**E**dit the Credit Message. This is independent of the Aging Messages option on the Bill Format 2 View of Browse Client Information.

The Client Funds options, while more involved, are better for handling advanced deposit or minimum retainers because they allow you to segregate the client funds and track their comings and goings separately. The flat retainer is treated like a flat fee and will be explained at the end of this chapter.

Before using the Client Funds Options, I strongly recommend that you change the default transaction phrases as described on page 97.

Timeslips refers to retainer or escrow monies as "Client Funds." If you prefer to track trust, retainer, or escrow funds separately from client payments, you need to set options on the **Balances & Funds** and **Bill Format 2** panels of that client's information screen. The Balances and Funds panel (See Figure 39) covers how the money will be applied to current fees and disbursements. The Bill Format 2 screen determines how this information will print on the client's bill. First, we will review the Client Funds Options on the Client Information Screen.

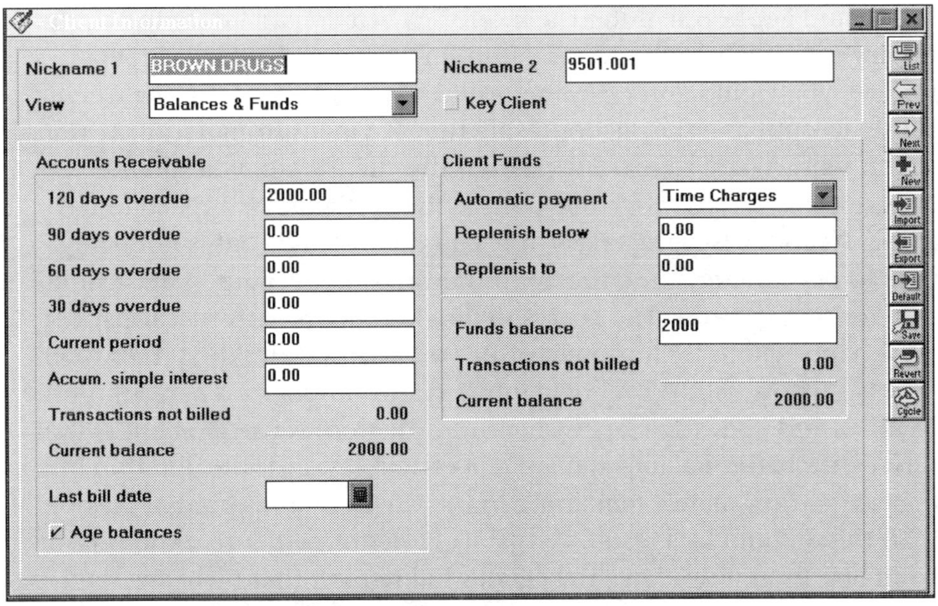

FIGURE 39. Client Information: Balances & Funds View

The Automatic Payment options are available by clicking the down arrow. You will be presented with the options: None, Time Charges, Expense, or Time & Expenses.

The Automatic Payment option lets you automatically apply the monies entered as "Payment to Account" or "Deposit to Account" under Transactions to the current time, the current disbursements, or both. Do not use Automatic Payment after you have already begun to bill the client. It will not apply against a previous balance. Also, be careful using this option if you tend to adjust all new charges or are billing the client on a flat fee that covers both time and expense. In these two situations, Timeslips will consider the entire bill as time, rather than time and costs, and will apply the adjustment to the entire bill.

The alternative to using the Automatic Payment option is to control the flow of money in and out of the Client Funds account completely through Transactions. For example, the initial money received on account from your client would be entered using the "Payment to Account" Transaction Type. For clarity, you might want to change the description for this transaction to "Retainer Received" or "Escrow Funds Received," depending on your type of practice. If the money you receive comes from a source other than your client, you should use the "Deposit to Account" option to enter the money. When you are ready to transfer money from the retainer to your firm, in exchange for services performed, you would enter the amount to be withdrawn from the Client Funds account as a transaction using the "Payment from Account" transaction type. Again, to make it clear on the client's bill, you should change the description for this transaction to "Retainer applied to Balance." If money is being taken from the Client Funds but is not being used to pay legal fees, use the "Withdrawal from Account" transaction type for that amount. The goal is to provide clients with a clear path of what happened to their money while your firm was holding it for them.

The "Replenish below" field, underneath Automatic Payment on the Balances and Funds screen of Client Information, is used to require that the client's Funds Balance remain at a certain level for the duration of the case. If the balance remaining in the Client's Funds becomes less than this amount as a result of legal work performed during the current billing cycle, you can have the client's bill request that he or she send in additional payment to maintain the minimum balance you would like to keep in their escrow or trust account during the transaction.

"Replenish to" lets clients know how much you would like to keep in their Client Funds account during their legal work. The difference between the amount you enter in the "Replenish to" field and the current funds balance will be the amount that will be requested in the Replenish message on the client's bill.

The Replenish options are used in conjunction with the options on the Bill Format 2 screen, where you should check the "replenish message" box so that clients will be told to submit the amount requested in the "Replenish to" box to keep their funds account from falling below the "Replenish below" amount.

Many lawyers have found that they have a better collection rate and fewer accounts receivable problems by maintaining a retainer account on behalf of a client and requiring it to stay at a predetermined level until the end of the legal work they are doing for the client.

The other option on the Bill Format 2 panel (see Figure 44 on page 136) concerning client funds allows you to show each individual transaction affecting client funds or simply a two-line summary of the activity. You should make your selection depending on your needs and how much information you need to relay to your clients.

Whether you are using Automatic Payment or applying it yourself, you should use the "Payment to Account" option to record payments that are to be segregated into the Client Funds account for that client. When you have entered an amount in the program as a Payment to Account, you will see the amount displayed on the Balance and Funds view of Client Information next to the field labeled "Funds Balance." If you use Automatic Payment, any amounts entered here will automatically be applied from the client's funds against legal work performed when you finalize a bill.

Flat Fees and Monthly Retainers

The only real difference between a one-time flat fee and an on-going monthly retainer is the duration. The flat fee is billed once while a monthly retainer goes on, hopefully, in perpetuity. The method for billing both of these is virtually identical.

The main focus for setting up flat fees or monthly retainers is the **Flat Fee & Hold** panel of Client Information. On the **Flat Fee & Hold** panel of Client Information, you can choose the Type of Flat Fee. An **Absolute Flat Fee** is one where, regardless of the amount of work represented by the individual time and/or disbursement slips for this case, the amount entered here will be the amount of the bill. The other types of flat fees are used less frequently.

A **Minimum Flat Fee** is one in which the amount of the flat fee will be charged even if the amount accrued on slips is less than the minimum amount. Any slips that bring the fees above the minimum will be added to the total due. A **Maximum Flat Fee** is a cap; after it is reached, no more fees will be billed. Until the Maximum Flat Fee is reached, the fees continue to be charged based on the amount represented in the actual time slips. You would typically use a Maximum Flat Fee in conjunction with the Job option under Duration until the Maximum amount is reached. When the Maximum amount is reached, you would need to manually change the Duration to Completed. A **Base Flat Fee** is one in which a specified amount needs to be billed each time a bill is rendered. Unlike a Minimum Flat Fee, however, all of the time and/or expense slips are added to the Base Flat Fee.

The **Contingency Flat Fee** option allows you to show the work being done for the client on bills during the case without a dollar amount being associated with them until the end of the case. When you select to bill a Contingency Flat Fee, you have a status field that is initially set to "In Progress." When the end of the case is reached, you change the Status field to "Final." If the amount you are to receive is a percentage of the judgment, you can use the Calculate button to determine the amount to be billed. Otherwise, you can simply enter the amount your firm is due in the Amount Field.

The **Percent Complete** option is helpful to Immigration lawyers and those who tend to break down the work they do for clients into discrete steps or phases. For example, obtaining a visa might represent the first occasion to present a bill for a fixed amount. This option presents you with a calculation work sheet to describe each of the phases and what percent of the total fee due they represent. Percent Complete bills are limited to time charges only.

To avoid complications and less common situations, we will focus on Absolute Flat Fees, since they are the most frequently used in small law offices. Once we have selected Absolute as our Type of flat fee, we are presented with the choices of whether to have the flat fee cover Time Charges only, Expense Charges only, Time and Expenses Combined or Separated. It is recommended that you choose Separated when you are preparing a flat fee bill where the amount will cover both so that you can better track the attorney's contribution to the work performed. These options will depend on the type of case and arrangement you have with your client. Next you will need to decide the Duration.

If you are working on a Real Estate closing or a Will Execution, the Duration should be set on Number of Bills with the # of Bills field using one (1). This means there will be a single bill with the amount specified to cover the time and/or expenses selected. Your Duration should be set on Perpetual if each time you prepare a bill for the client, you want to bill the same amount.

The Amount entered in the Amount field will depend, in part, on the particular type of flat fee you are using. With the exception of the Absolute Perpetual flat fee, the amount will be the amount for the entire case. The Absolute Perpetual flat fee, which is really a monthly or quarterly retainer, should be the amount for each billing cycle.

The Flat Fee Message box gives you a place to describe the work you are doing in exchange for the flat fee. If you are preparing a single bill where you do not want to show the information actually entered on the individual slips or are billing regularly for a set amount, you should enter the description you want to appear on the bill in this Flat Fee message area. You will then need to limit the options selected on the Bill Format 1 view to avoid having information from the actual slips also appear on the bill. Several of the Flat Fee arrangements allow you to include more information on the bill, as shown in the lower left-hand corner of Bill Format 1.

Additionally, there is also the option, when charging a flat fee, to indicate that certain time or expense slips should be added to the flat fee. This could be helpful in a situation where you are getting a monthly retainer but are permitted to charge above that amount for work done in court on the client's behalf. Your other option in this situation would be to set up the client under two different nicknames and track the work separately.

As an example, you are sending a one-time, flat-fee bill for a real estate closing, you would select:

Type: Absolute

Covers: Time Only

Duration: Number of Bills

# of Bills: 1

Description: Paragraph to describe your work.

On the Bill Format 1 view, you would then choose:

Time Style: Totals Only

Expense Style: Itemize or Activity Summary (depends on your preferences)

You would probably want to limit the options selected under Time Charges, although you might include some of the ones under Expenses since the typical real estate closing includes expenses billed separately from the legal fee. To understand the options on the Bill Format 1 screen, you should refer to the Chapter on Bill Layout.

Getting Information to Help You Analyze Your Retainers and Flat Fees

There are a number of reports that will help you determine whether you are truly profiting from charging flat fees for your work.

The **Full Detail Billing Worksheet** will give you an analysis for a specific client.

The **Client Funds** report will assist you in monitoring the comings and goings of funds in your Client Funds accounts. Be sure to review the choices under Options before running this report.

Flat Fee Performance under the Client WIP Report compares the flat fees to the actual time and expenses entered on behalf of your clients.

Finally, the **User Contribution Report** may assist you in looking at the work each lawyer in the firm is doing to improve the firm's profits.

Although the options for handling retainers may seem daunting, the flexibility that Timeslips provides in accommodating different flat-fee, retainer, and escrow situations more than compensates for the time investment in learning how and when to use them.

CHAPTER SEVEN

Setting Up Timeslips

Create a New Database

During the installation of Timeslips, the setup program will take you through the steps to create a new database. If you are upgrading from an earlier version of Timeslips, the first time you try to access information in your database, Timeslips will look for any existing databases and give you the opportunity to upgrade them.

As part of the creation of a new database, you will be asked whether you want to use one of the preset Professions databases as the basis for your new database. The "Lawyer" profession database will assign terminology, activity codes for time activities and expenses, abbreviations, and custom client fields. Depending on how closely your firm matches the predefined fields, you may find that you are better off creating your own activities, abbreviations, and custom client fields rather than having to eliminate or edit the ones that come with the Lawyer profession database and the Legal-ABA Litigation Task Codes. If you need to prepare bills with the ABA Uniform Task Based Litigation Codes, you should select Legal-ABA Litigation Task Codes. Choose Standard Database to set up your own codes.

Terminology

If you select Standard database, or want to change the labels for your database, you will be asked to assign the Terminology you want to use. (You can always change these labels once the database has been created by selecting **S**ETTINGS/**T**erminology, although if you change your Client.Project separator once you have begun to set up clients, you will have to edit all of the client nicknames to update them.)

Terminology allows you to change the labels that you will see as you are working through the program. Use this option to change the labels USER, CLIENT, and ACTIVITY as suggested below:

From	To
User	Attorney
Client	Client.Matter
Activity	Time/$Disb
Reference	Case Reference
Project	Matter

Depending on the codes you use for clients and matters, you may want to change the client label so that it matches the structure you are using. For example, if your firm uses a client's last name and first initial as one of its client nicknames, you might want to change the label to CLIENT LASTF to remind people how to enter client names. Since Activity is used for time codes and disbursements, I prefer to change the Activity label to read TIME/$DISB. This also reminds people that Expense codes start with a $.

The Private Text indicator is a character that you can assign to let Timeslips know when you are adding information to a slip description, payment, or message that you do not want to print on a client's bill. To separate text that you would want to print on a client's bill as part of either a slip description or payment description from text that you just want to track internally, I suggest you use an exclamation point as your private text indicator, since an exclamation point (!) is rarely used in legal time descriptions or payment descriptions and is easy to remember and use when you want it as private text. When you are done with the terminology screen, click on **OK**.

Update Capacity

During installation, Timeslips will also ask you to determine your initial Capacity settings. While it is tempting to simply select the maximum numbers allowed for each category, you should not go overboard on these. Essentially, you are reserving space on your hard drive for the capacity you do not yet need. The Attorney field should be set for one or two more timekeepers than you have in the firm, if your version of Timeslips can accommodate it. Depending on how often you add new cases, you should anticipate about six months' worth of new matters.

You can always update the capacity when you run low. In fact, you should monitor this number periodically by looking under File/Update Capacity. The Activity (TIME/$DISB) field should be set for about ten more codes than you are using. If you do not know how many activities you will be using, leave it set on 40 and review this later.

Operational Preferences

If you are setting up Timeslips from scratch with a brand new database, you will need to do some one-time setups. If you have an existing database, you may want to review the settings discussed in this section to ensure that you have used them well in connection with your firm's needs. Even if you have been using Timeslips for a while, you may want to review these instructions to be sure your firm is taking advantage of the shortcuts and tips I have included here.

To start, click on the SETTINGS icon on the Navigator. This will display the SETTINGS Panel. If you are more inclined to use the pull-down menus, you can select **S**ETTINGS/**O**perational. The first section you want to examine is called Operational Preferences, which lets you define preset options for how you are going to handle new clients and new cases. The changes you make here affect only new cases, not existing ones.

Billing Rates

Most law firms who charge their clients based on hourly rates bill out their timekeepers based on their position in the firm. Senior partners charge higher hourly rates than junior ones. Attorneys bill at higher rates than paralegals. Rate Source in the Operational Preferences is where you tell Timeslips to assume you are billing based on the attorneys' hourly rates. Rate Source should be set to *Attorney* and Rate Level should be *1*. When you set up each client (see page 138), you will have the option of overriding this setting for a specific client.

If, however, you are a sole practitioner or an insurance defense firm, you might have different billing rates based on whom the *client* is rather than the *timekeeper*. Sole practitioners should use *Client* as the Rate Source, since there is only one timekeeper and the rate will depend on the particular arrangement with each client. Many insurance defense firms bill at a set rate for the carrier regardless of the level of the employee who is doing the work. If this fits your situation, you should also use *Client* as the Rate Source.

> ➤TIP: If you have a variation of the two, you might consider using *Client* as the Rate Source and use Level 1 for partners, Level 2 for associates, and Level 3 for paralegals. In this scenario, the people entering time need to change levels when they are entering time for people other than the partners, but they will generally know the position of the person in the firm for whom they are entering time and will not need to remember which rate applies to which person and which carrier.

If you are using Attorney as the Rate Source, you will enter the actual rates for each timekeeper as you set up the Attorneys. See page 120. If you are using Client as the Rate Source, you will enter the Client rate as you set up each Client.

> ➤TIP: You may also want to enter an Attorney Rate for each timekeeper so that you can run comparison reports to see what you would have received at your regular billing rate compared with the rate you are actually billing.

To complete the rest of the options on this screen, you must understand the concept of a key client.

Key Clients and the Options for Handling Clients and Matters

There are three different ways to handle clients and matters in Timeslips. Each has advantages and disadvantages. The first and simplest approach is a single client with a single matter. In essence, each matter is a client in the program. We will refer to this method as "Single Client, Single Matter." The advantages of this approach are that each matter is wholly contained with its own Client Information screen, payments and adjustments, and bill format, you have easier coding, you can control information at the matter level, and you can enter payments at the matter level. The disadvantages are that you cannot group the matters for billing purposes and you cannot get client level reports and totals. To set up, you simply create a new client nickname for each new case.

The second way to handle matters is set up a "Single Client with Multiple Matters." Timeslips refers to this as "Client.Project." This is the method that uses the "key" client options. You would use this option when you have a major client with different types of matters that need to be handled differently or where you want to track payments at the matter level. For instance, you may be handling a client's divorce and at the same time handling his or her house sale. In order to designate a key client and subsequent matters, you first need to define your separator on the Terminology screen described on page 113.

The Key Client and its information screen serve as a template for the settings and options that you want for that client and new matters for that client. Insurance defense firms are a good example of the type of practice that would take advantage of the Client. Project format using a Key client. If a firm represented ABC Insurance Company, it would set up a Key Client called ABC. On the Client Information screens, all the options such as the address, the rate, the bill format, in terms of whether you want hours, amounts, description, and so on to show would be set for that Key Client. When a new matter needs to be set up, it might be ABC.001. By having the prefix ABC. and designating ABC. as a Key Client in combination with these Operational Settings, you can shortcut the data-entry process. On the Operational Settings screen, you can then tell Timeslips to use the bill format, the rate, the custom fields, and the name and address from your key client. This means you do not have to set these options individually as you create new matters for this client.

On the Operational Preferences screen, you can preset which other settings you want to be presumed when you set up the additional matters for a Key Client. Finally, when you actually set up the clients and their matters, you need to designate one of the client's matters as the Key Client and use consistent nicknames (a common prefix with your separator) for subsequent matters. The major advantages of this method of using Client are that you can decide on a matter-by-matter basis whether to bill each matter; what billing format and billing arrangements you want (such as flat fee, different billing rates, and so on), whether you want all or some of the matters to be billed together on a single bill, on separate pages, or as separate bills. You have the option to print a summary page of each of the matters broken down. You can also track the payments separately, and in your reports you can get both client and matter level totals.

To set up this style, you create a single client nickname for the client and complete the Client Information Screen. To set up the matters, highlight the client name on the Client List, choose References from the Will Open To dialog at the top of the screen, then click Open. You can then enter brief descriptions for each matter. When you prepare bills for clients set up this way, you should choose bill Sort by Reference as your Sort Option.

The fields on the Operational Preferences screen correspond to parts of the Client Information Screens for each client or matter, depending on your use of clients and matters as discussed above. If your firm uses the Single Client with Multiple Matters style, you can select which components you want to copy from the Key Client to the new matters here. Generally, you should be setting Bill Formats, Markup, Custom Fields, Name and Address, and Rates to *Key*. This means that new matters for the same Key Client will have the same bill format (dates, initials, hours, and so on), the same rounding options, the same Custom Client Fields, the same name and address, and the same billing rate. You can override any of these on an individual matter. The idea is to save time in setting up new matters.

If your firm does not use the Key Client method of organizing your clients and matters, you can use the predefined client "Your Company" as the template for new clients. In that event, you will want to set these options on the Operational Settings screen to Your Company. By setting Your Company in the Client Information Section to your firm's most common options, you can preset new clients and matters with the firm's standard settings and modify them on a case-by-case basis.

To select options on this screen you can click on the down triangle (▼), or if you are on an earlier version the down triangle that is underlined, and you will see the options available for each particular field. When you are done, click on **OK**.

The third way to handle clients and matters is what I call "Single Client with Related Matters." This method uses a defined Reference field and allows you to have all the matters broken down on the same bill. Billing only some matters is more difficult than with the Key Client screens but many firms prefer the format since it can sort by Reference with Subtotals and underline the Case Description Title above each section. This option seems to work especially well for landlord-tenant practices as well as employment law firms where there are multiple, similar matters in any billing cycle.

Personal Preferences

Most of the options found under Personal Preferences generally are acceptable to most people as they are installed. There are four view panels of personal preferences that you can select. Each person on a local area network can have his or her own settings on these screens. On the **Interface** view, you may want to choose to skip initial messages on startup and omit seeing the Timeslips logo when you start the main program. These will make the program open more quickly. The options associated with the **Navigator & Script Options** view are best left to advanced users. The choices in the **Backup Options** view will depend on how your system gets backed up. Whatever your method, be sure you are backing up your Timeslips data regularly. I recommend that you set Backup when exiting TSReport to Yes or Ask to back up to floppies in addition to a tape drive. Restoring a Timeslips database from diskettes is generally easier than from tape and provides you with an additional backup in the event of a problem. You should set the Print to file path in **Default File Path** to the directory location where you print your bills to a file. (If you are not sure where this is or have never set this up, consider creating a BILLS directory within your word processing file structure for this purpose. This way, if you need to access the file copies of your bills, they will be readily accessible in your word processor. The Temporary file path should be set to the same directory as your Windows temporary files. Usually, this is either C:\TEMP or C:\WINDOWS\TEMP. Periodically, you should remove any files that appear in that directory. (Make sure you are not running any programs when you delete temp files!)

> ►TIP: If you have upgraded from an earlier version of Timeslips, or if your computer crashed, you should look for any temporary files in your TSREPORT directory and remove them. These files will have file names like albpbbeg or alcaaacl, no file extension and will usually have 0 bytes or a small number. If you have not done this in a really long time, like never, you may have files that start with the letter B as well.

Security

Timeslips is very flexible in terms of security. It provides for a supervisor as well as group settings, which it refers to as Profiles. You can have separate profiles for the bookkeeper, the partners, and the associates and staff. For example, you might want to limit the associates and staff access to reports and prevent them from adding or changing client information. You can also make exceptions to the Group Profiles and set up individual profiles for specific users on the system.

As with any network software, you should set up someone as the Supervisor. I recommend that a second person be aware of the password as a backup in case of an emergency.

Financial Rules

Under Financial Settings, Timeslips is preset for aging your Accounts Receivable information by thirty, sixty, ninety, and 120 days. Unless you want to make changes to these settings, you do not need to go into the Financial Settings screen. Financial Settings also addresses tax method if your jurisdiction requires you to collect service tax on your professional services or if you sell products and need to charge sales tax for some of those products and want to incorporate that into your billing system. Otherwise, you can skip financial rules.

Create Attorney Nicknames and Rates

The timekeepers are set up by selecting **Names/Attorney Info**, or pressing **CTRL+U,** or using the Navigator screen (click on Attorney icon, which should be the picture with the three little people, and select New Attorney). If your system has been already set up for you, select Browse Attorney Information instead. Timeslips Deluxe lets you have two different nicknames to identify each timekeeper. The most common nickname is each attorney's initials. If you do not use the second nickname, Timeslips will assign it a unique number in sequence for each attorney or timekeeper being defined. If your firm also uses a numbering system, you can use Nickname 1 for the initials and Nickname 2 for the attorney number. If not, you might want to put the attorney's initials in as both Nickname 1 and 2 to avoid confusion and to allow the firm to switch back and forth between the two sets of nicknames without having to worry about which one is being displayed.

Below the nicknames is provision for six attorney rates. Timeslips allows you to have six separate rates for each timekeeper. If, as described under Operational Preferences on page 115, you are using the rate source as Attorney and Rate Level 1, you should put the rate that is most commonly used by each timekeeper as Rate 1 on this screen. You will see that as you set up additional timekeepers, their Rate 1 should also be their most commonly used rate for the firm. When you set up clients, you can designate which Rate Level to pull from for each of the attorneys. For instance, if I am the partner, when I am charging my Rate 1, the associate and paralegal on the same matter should also be charging their Rate 1. When I am charging my Rate 3, which may be a lower rate, they should also be charging their Rate 3 from their information screen.

The Overhead Rate allows you to track an hourly rate that you pay to an employee or subcontractor for the work they perform on your firm's behalf. For example, you may be billing a paralegal at a rate of $50 per hour to a client. That would be entered as Rate 1. However, if you are paying that paralegal $30 per hour, you would enter that as his overhead rate. The Attorney Overhead Cost Report will let you compare what you are paying as opposed to what your clients are paying for that service by each timekeeper.

Under Other Information, enter the attorney's initials as you would want them to appear next to slip information on bills and enter his or her full name below that. The full name information can be used as part of the rate table on bills, selected on Bill Format 2 screen within Client Information. Since you have thirty-five characters in the full name field, you may wish to put in something like "Carol Schlein, Partner" so that the rate table, if you use it on your bills, is more clear as to the level of employee who did the work for the client.

When you are ready to enter an additional timekeeper, you can simply select **NEW** from the buttons on the right-hand side of the screen or press **CTRL+N**. This will automatically save the first person's information and start you with a new screen to set up the next timekeeper. When you are all finished, you can use the shortcut key, **CTRL+W,** to have Timeslips return you to the Main Navigator screen.

> ►TIP: One of my favorite tips is to create an attorney whose nickname is "Disbursements" with no rates, no initials, and no full name necessary to complete. Unless your clients require an attorney's name associated with the disbursements they created, you can enter all the disbursement slips under this timekeeper whose nickname is Disbursements. By doing this, you simplify selecting slips for reports later in the process. For example, if you want to exclude all the different types of disbursements from a report, simply excluding the timekeeper named Disbursements will remove disbursement information from the given report. Similarly, to create a report that includes only disbursements of a variety of types, you can simply select the attorney named Disbursements and not have to select the individual types of disbursements to create the report.

To print out a report or a list of the attorneys and their rates to verify the information from the Navigator panel for Attorney, you can select the Information Listing box and print it to the printer. On the pull-down menu, you can select REPORTS/3 Attorney/Nickname Listing.

Create Activity Codes

Activity is the term Timeslips uses to describe both time and expense nickname codes when entering slips. There are two different approaches you can take to using the Activity codes for time entry. The first is to keep things simple and use only a few Activity codes for time entry and rely on the Abbreviations feature to enter descriptions quickly. The other option is to define your time activities with the beginning of a description in the activity definition. The Timeslips manual assumes you will have separate activities for each major task you perform. Similarly, if you chose to use one of the Lawyer databases when you installed the program, you will have a large group of activities with descriptions that may or may not suit your firm's preference.

For most lawyers, these activities tend to be confusing and more complicated than they need be. Additionally, they can be used to create reports that are virtually useless for most law firms. Very few lawyers care to see a report that shows how much time they spent talking on the telephone with clients as opposed to writing correspondence. Unless you have a specific need, such as for task-based billing, as discussed below, or need to establish flat rates for specific legal activities using the Rate Override tables in Client Information, or are linking to a case-management program such as Time Matters for Windows ™, Amicus Attorney Team™, or Abacus Law for Windows™, I suggest that you keep the number of time activities to a minimum. You can use either TIME or SERVICES to identify your billable work. Your other time codes might include: "Nonbillable," "No Charge," "Client Developt," "Admin.", "Vacation" and "Misc."

Some firms charge different rates for different legal work, such as work performed in court as opposed to work done in other locations. If your firm has a special in-court rate, you should create an "In Court" activity. When you establish the client's rate, you can attach an "override default rate" to let the program know that when it sees the In Court rate on a time slip, it should apply the special rules for that rate.

Task-Based Billing Considerations

One of the main exceptions to using a minimum number of time codes is for law firms whose clients require them to track their billing by client-defined tasks. More and more corporate clients of law firms are adopting the American Bar Association's Uniform Task-Based Management System:

Litigation Code Set. They require their outside counsel to identify each legal activity with specific codes tied to the phases and tasks involved in litigation or corporate representation.

There are several problems with task-based billing. First, no two auditing companies or law firm clients has the same requirements. This means that you may have to produce different information for each client that requires task-based billing codes. Second, the current versions of Timeslips is limited to 250 Activity Codes, 255 Abbreviations, and 128 References. The ABA list include more codes than there is room for in Timeslips. This means you must forgo your own codes and limit the ABA list to the codes you are most likely to use. This will hopefully be resolved in the next version of Timeslips.

If you are starting from scratch, choose the Legal-ABA Litigation Task Codes to set up these codes when you install Timeslips. If you need to add them or edit your existing codes, look at the format used in Appendix C. If you are required to submit task-based bills, you should enter each task as its own activity. Depending on the particular format the client requires, you may also need to use the "Reference" portion of the program to group the various activities by their respective phases.

Often, the client requires the law firm to submit billing information in a particular format to a third party that reviews and analyzes the bill and determines whether the firm will get paid for its work, and if so, how much. These companies are looking for double and inappropriate billing from the law firms. More and more corporate clients are turning to task-based billing as a way to control outside legal costs. To continue to respond to their corporate clients' needs, these third-party auditing firms are adding more requirements, such as defining the actual text that will be associated with each task code. This will allow these companies to provide additional analysis to their corporate clients.

The task-based codes are intended to assist corporate counsel in monitoring outside counsel's work based on specific groupings of legal service tasks. The litigation codes are grouped into five basic phases of litigation plus expenses: Case Assessment, Development and Administration; Pre-Trial Pleadings and Motions; Discovery; Trial Preparation and Trial; and Appeal. Each phase consists of various tasks such as Written Discovery, Document Production, and so on. Many corporate clients require the use of these codes as well as the submission of bills in a particular format on diskette. Timeslips is working very closely with the auditing companies that are collecting and analyzing the bills to ensure that Timeslips can easily prepare the required formats. While there is general acceptance of the actual codes, there is currently little agreement about the format of the information that needs to be submitted for payment on legal work.

The Activity nicknames were enhanced in Timeslips 7 to better accommodate the requirements for task-based billing. Additionally, Timeslips Corporation has made arrangements with Legalgard, one of the auditing companies, and has add-on modules for Versions 7 and 8 that prepare Timeslips bills in formats acceptable to Legalgard and its clients. (Even different Legalgard clients have different formats. It's far from uniform.) If you are using Timeslips 6 and have clients who require you to bill by task-specific codes, you may want to upgrade. The difficulty for some firms is that they may have number codes for the clients who demand task-based bills and a different system for their other clients. If this is the case for your firm, you should consider taking advantage of the second nickname available in Timeslips Version 6 and above. In this scenario, you can use your firm's preferred system as nickname 1 and the corresponding task-based codes as nickname 2 for overlapping activities. When printing reports for the clients who require task-based bills, simply select the second nickname for those bills.

Entering Time Activity Nicknames

Start from NAMES/Activity Info (or whatever label you are using for Activity), or from the Activity panel of the Navigator select New Time Activity or Browse Activity Information and then New, or use the shortcut key **CTRL+Y** and then click on the Time button on the right-hand side of the dialog box. Figure 40 shows the Time Activity Information Screen.

You will have the option of having two different nicknames for each activity. If you cannot think of some way to use the second nickname, I would suggest putting the same code in twice so that you do not see the unique numbers that Timeslips generates if you leave it blank. This number tends to confuse new users. If you had numbers in a previous billing system for these codes, you might want to enter those as Nickname 2.

Version 7 added a new field, Full Name, which you can use as part of your bill format. This is more useful for disbursements than time codes in a law firm environment. However, it can also be used to make data entry of task-based codes easier. For example, you might be required to enter L350 - Discovery Motions as your task code on the bill, but the lawyers in the firm find it easier to use codes such as DSM on their time slips. Additionally, this extra field can be useful for firms who have some clients who require the task-based codes and others who don't but want

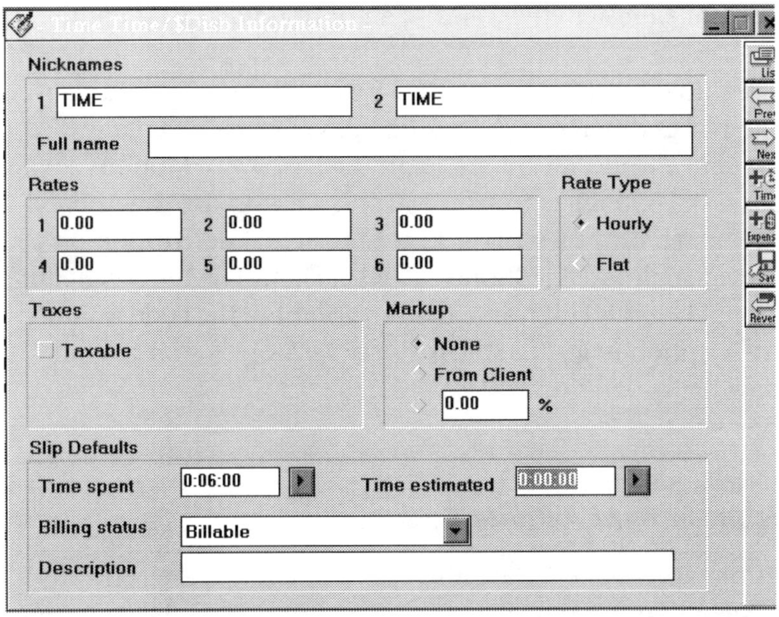

FIGURE 40. Time Activity Codes Entry Screen

a single, unified list of activity codes. The Full Name field can also serve as the translation of the code for the bill itself depending on the firm's need. Additionally, there is also a personal set of abbreviations that individuals within the firm can use. However, it is advisable to establish some firm-wide conventions for more consistent client bills.

For time-based codes, you will not generally charge tax or markup your work. Unless you have special rates for specific activities, you do not have to set any rates here, since your rates are going to be determined by either who the attorney is or who the client is, depending on your practice. If you prefer, you can set the time spent as a minimum of 1/10 of an hour by typing in ".1" in the Time Spent field. You will see this converted automatically to six minutes when you create your time slips. Later on, when you do reports and create bills, it will be converted back to tenths. To save time when you are entering time slips, you should set your billing status as Billable.

If you are going to use "TIME" as the nickname for most of your entries, you will not want a preset description on this screen. You can press **CTRL+S** (SAVE), click the Save icon, or select the Time icon on the right-hand side to create a new time nickname.

Create any other time-related nicknames that you need for your firm. You have fifteen characters to describe each activity so you will have to abbreviate some of them. Again, you can now use the Full Name field to further explain your time activities, and as an option you can then use on your bills.

If you are required by clients to do task-based billing, you would enter your time activities differently. For example, your first nickname might be L350, your second nickname might be Discovery Motions so you know what task L350 refers to. You will still want to use the Abbreviation feature discussed on pages 131–133 for the actual description of the task performed such as "Telephone call with client regarding scheduling of deposition." Use the Full Name field to combine the code number and required description (e.g., "L350 Discovery Motions") so it is available for billing.

Entering Disbursement Activity Codes

Disbursements or expenses codes are also entered here but are generally simpler to do. Keep in mind that Timeslips does not distinguish between costs advanced and disbursements, which other billing systems sometimes do. If you need to account for this, you might consider how you label your disbursements so that they can be grouped accordingly.

If you have just finished entering time codes, you can start entering your expense codes from the same screen by clicking on the Expense button on the right-hand side of the Information screen. If you took a break from setting up your system or want to add new expense codes, you can press **CTRL+Y** and then click the Expense button. When you do this, you will notice that Timeslips automatically inserted a dollar sign (**$**) on both nickname 1 and nickname 2. This is how Timeslips distinguishes between time- and expense-related slips. To set up an expense activity for filing fees, you would type in the nickname "Filing Fee" at the insertion point. Depending on how your firm uses the second nickname option, you will type in either the same information or you can put in a number or some other way to cross-reference this particular nickname. This might be a handy way to match your disbursement information to codes used in conjunction with your telephone system, photocopiers or any other charge-back device.

If you are using the task-based billing codes for your clients, you might use a familiar name description as one nickname (Photocopies) and the task code (e.g., E100) as the other.

When entering your nicknames for activities, you should make them as clear as possible in case you want to use a bill format that summarizes your expenses by type. In other words, use Photocopies instead of Copies and Long Distance instead of LDT. Timeslips 7 added a new field, Full Name, which is especially useful for tracking disbursements and making them clearer on clients' bills. For example, you might have an expense for photocopies. The activity nickname is limited to fifteen characters including the required dollar sign. Your code might be $COPIES. However, on the bill you would like the client to see the words "Photocopies at $.15 per page." Prior to Version 7, you would need to use the Description for each slip and summarize the slips (a tedious task that required you to create a new slip for each client and each activity that you want billed in this manner). With the option of the Full Name field in Version 7, you can enter this description as the Full Name and use the "Summarize by Activity" format for your expenses. See page 136 for a discussion of how to set up this bill format option.

If, in your jurisdiction, the particular service you are rendering is taxable, you should check the taxable box. This will tie back to the Tax, Interest, and Markup View of the Client Information screen. On the right-hand side you have markup information. This allows you to add a percent onto the actual cost of the expense either from the client information screen or at a set percent for this particular transaction. Some firms charge a percent markup on services such as on-line legal research, although the use of this seems to be declining due to client pressure. In this case, you are not going to mark up your photocopies. Be careful to comply with your jurisdiction's ethics guidelines.

At the bottom of the screen you have slip defaults. These are the preset pieces of information that you would like to show up automatically when you are creating a new expense slip. Most firms that charge for photocopying have a set rate per page. Enter your firm's per page or per unit rate for each type of disbursement that requires it. This allows you, when you are creating your slip, simply to enter the number of copies and the number of fax pages transmitted and let Timeslips do the math to multiply the quantity times the price. Disbursements such as filing fees do not have a preset price in most jurisdictions. As with the time-entry codes, you can have the billing status preset as well. Again, you can use Billable as your preset option for billing status.

Attaching a description to each disbursement nickname will save time when you are entering disbursement slips. This will also allow you to switch to a more itemized bill format after the information has been entered without much fuss. For example, entering the term "Filing Fees" as your description here means that when you create a slip for filing fees in the time-entry portion of the program, the slip will automatically already say "Filing Fees." You can add to that description or change it, but this is what will show up without any other steps being taken.

If you are going to add another new expense activity nickname, select the Expense icon on the right-hand side of the screen. If you are finished, you can either select save on the right-hand side or press the shortcut key **CTRL+W** and it will ask, "Do you want to save the changes made to this activity?" to which you should respond "yes."

> ➤TIP: The Lawyer database includes fifteen predefined activity nicknames for expenses. If you have used the Lawyer option on a new database, you will want to add or change the codes or descriptions for each of the expense types that you use as well as edit the nicknames to match better the types of expenses that you use in your firm as well as their rates when applicable.

To print out the list of time and expense nicknames as well as their rates and associated information, you can either select REPORTS/4 Activity/Nickname Listing or from the Navigator select the Activity section and go to Information Listing.

Custom Client Fields

Timeslips allows you to define fifteen Custom Client fields whose information can be attached to each client or matters information screen. Earlier versions of Timeslips support three different types of custom fields: text, user, and list. Timeslips Deluxe 6.0 and above support a date field. These fields are useful in preparing reports and sorting information and are often overlooked by new users and upgraders alike. For example, you could create a "user" field for Responsible Attorney. This would allow you to print bills sorted by who reviews the case. You could also use this field to get subtotals of client billing information. Similarly, you can create a "list" field for area of law and get reports that give you work performed or dollars collected for each of your firm's practice areas. Starting with Version 6, List fields are also helpful in grouping clients together for billing cycles or reports. You can also prepare a client name and address list of clients who were new to the firm this year by using the "date" field information to select only those clients added since the first of this year. Finally, you can attach important information about clients to their information screens using the "text" field. For instance, you might want to know who referred the client to your firm.

►TIP TEXT: A Text Field is used to store specific information that is unique each time it is entered. You have up to thirty characters available. Text fields cannot be used for selecting or sorting on bills and reports but can be printed out or viewed in the Client Information screen. A good example of a text field would be "Referred By," where your referral sources vary.

USER: This type of Custom Field allows you to group clients by particular attorney or timekeeper in the firm as a way to sort or select specific cases when you are creating reports or compiling information. For example, you may wish to create a custom field for the billing attorney. In Settings, you create these specific custom fields. When you move over to the Client's Information screen, you will actually assign a specific timekeeper or partner to each particular client and matter.

LIST: List is one of the most powerful options available for Custom Fields. In Settings, you can define a list of options that can be tied to a specific field. Good examples would include Case Type and Billing Cycle. If your firm handles a selected set of practice areas, you would define each of those as part of the list. Again, when you set up the specific case, you would then pick from this list for that particular case.

DATE: Date is a new option with Timeslips Deluxe that allows you to associate a date with a specific case or matter. For example, you may wish to have a Date Opened and a Date Closed field so that you can run reports or do analysis based on when cases or client matters were opened and when they were closed.

How to Create Custom Client Fields

If you selected the Lawyer database when you created your new database, you will already have a number of custom fields defined for you. Highlight any of the fields you do not need and press the delete button underneath the list to remove any custom fields that you do not want to keep. You can also edit them by highlighting the label and making changes to it in the window below the list of fields. If you have a field highlighted, you can use the up and down buttons to change its order in the list so that these flow in a logical order based on how you're going to input information into your firm's data.

Figure 41 below shows typical custom fields.

The New button lets you create a new custom field. If you did not use the legal installation option or have deleted most of the options that were there and want to define your own, you will start with New. You will use Insert when you want to add a new field above the currently highlighted field.

When you click on New, your cursor will move to the title field. Title is the label that you want to see when you're in your client's information screen next to the field. You have fifteen characters to define the field. Unless you are a sole practitioner, the first field that you may want to see on your list will be Billing Attorney. Type "Billing Attorney" as the title, then use the tab key to move over to Type and select user (or timekeeper) here. Click on Accept once you have completed these steps.

Creating a Date or Text Field is similar to creating a timekeeper or user field. Creating a List Field is more involved. Again, you define the title, for instance, Case Type. Under Type you will tell Timeslips that it is a List Field. You will then see an Open List Entries button below the type area which will allow you to create your specific list that relates to this particular field. Figure 42 shows a sample list for case types.

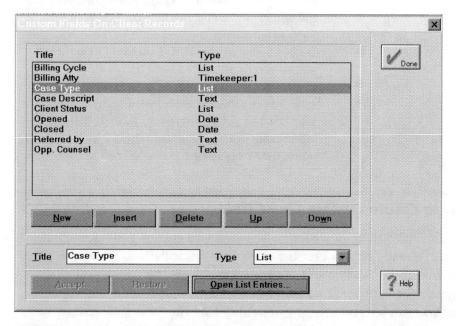

FIGURE 41. Settings: Custom Client Fields Screen

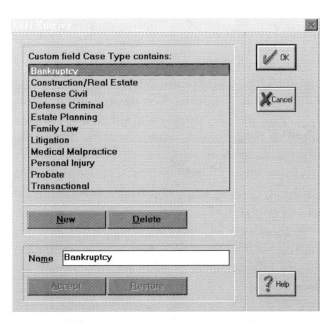

FIGURE 42. Settings: Custom Client Fields: List Types Sample Screen

For Case Type, you might include real estate, litigation, personal injury, etc. Again, use New to create, Accept to save, and click on OK when you have completed your particular list for the specific custom field you are creating. When you have completed your custom fields, labels, and list entries, click on Done.

Abbreviations

Abbreviations are shortcuts for commonly used phrases that you use to describe your time. For example, you may have "TCC" as a shortcut for "telephone call to client concerning" or "MW" for "meeting with." If your firm does not currently have a set of abbreviations, you may want to start by looking at your existing bills for commonly used phrases that your firm uses in preparing bills. It is important that the lawyers review the proposed list of abbreviations and agree on basic phrases such as "telephone call with" or "telephone conference with." The attorneys should also review the proposed abbreviations so that they will be more inclined to use the abbreviations on their written time sheets if they are recording their time on paper instead of directly on the computer.

In designing your firm's abbreviations, you should keep in mind how these get used in the time-entry screen. Your abbreviations should consist of *at least* two letters and not consist of any real words such as RE or TO. You should limit the quantity of abbreviations you have so that they are usable and easily recalled by the lawyers when they are entering their time.

Version 7 enhanced the abbreviation function by allowing you to insert prompts inside your abbreviations. If your favorite phrase is "telephone call to XXX, Esq." you can now set up the abbreviation so it pauses for you to put in the opposing counsel's name and then have the abbreviation complete the phrase.

From the pull-down menu, select **S**ETTINGS/**C**ustom Text/**A**bbreviations. If you are using the Navigator, select the Abbreviations button on the Settings Panel or just press **F7**.

To create a new abbreviation, click on **New,** your insertion point will be in the Abbreviation field. You should enter your abbreviation here; for example TCC. Hit the Tab key to go to meaning and type in "telephone call with client concerning."

> ►TIP: If you start the Meaning portion of your Abbreviation with a lowercase letter, you will have the option when you are using the abbreviation in your slips to start your phrase with either an uppercase or lowercase letter. For example, when you enter the description for your time, if you type in **Tcc** and press any piece of punctuation, this expands to read "Telephone call with client concerning." However, if you type in the abbreviation as lowercase **tcc**, this will translate as "telephone call with client concerning."

If you are using Version 7 or above, you can insert a pause into the meaning of the abbreviation. At the location where you want to insert the prompt, simply click on the Insert Prompt box below your description area. Timeslips will let you type a brief prompt (this is the message you will see on the screen when it pauses to let you fill in the blank). If you wanted to enhance your "tcc" code above, you might substitute a prompt for the word client so that you can fill in the actual client's name. Timeslips will surround the prompt with percent (%) signs. If you prefer, you can have several prompts in the same abbreviation. This feature was added for firms that are required to do task-based billing and are now being asked to use more specific formats for the text of their descriptions. Ironically, it is really handy for the rest of us.

Click on Done when you are finished adding abbreviations. Once you have your basic set of abbreviations, you can also add new abbreviations on the fly while you are entering time or expense slips. This, however, can result in overlapping abbreviations if you're not careful to verify what abbreviations are already in the system. If you want to print a list of the abbreviations and their meanings from the system, select REPORTS/5 System/Abbreviations.

Timeslips 7 also adds the ability to have a firm set of abbreviations as well as individual ones. Simply click on the Database or Personal tab to create the set of abbreviations. When you are entering your slips, both the firm's database and your personal abbreviations are available. There are a number of clever ways to take advantage of this feature. For instance, you might have firm abbreviations that use numbers and personal ones that translate them into mnemonic abbreviations. Another situation might be where you have to use specific abbreviations and phrases for certain clients but prefer other abbreviations for others.

If you used the Lawyer database or task-based option to set a new database, you will already have a number of abbreviations to use when entering your timeslips. You can simply highlight one of those phrases and edit that abbreviation or its meaning, which is what it will expand to when you use it in your slips in this screen. Alternatively, you can delete the unwanted abbreviations.

Setting Up Clients

Now that you have told Timeslips about your attorneys and the types of codes you are going to use, you can set up your clients and matters.

Your Company

The Your Company screen is where you set up the firm-wide options. You may recall that you had the option in Operational Preferences (discussed on page 115, to have Timeslips look to Your Company as the template for setting up new clients.

Depending on your mood, can access the Your Company screen four different ways: you can choose NAMES/Client Info or Press **CTRL+I** or click on the BILL CYCLE or CLIENT panel of the Navigator and choose Browse Client Information, highlight Your Company, and click on Open. If you click on the SETTINGS Panel and choose the Company Address and Client Defaults box, you are taken automatically into the Name and Address view of Your Company.

Company Address and Client Defaults

Type in your firm name and address, which can be used in bills at the top of letterhead and will appear across the top of internal reports.

On the right-hand side of this screen and on many of the Timeslips screens, you'll see a tool bar with shortcut buttons. These buttons allow you to quickly move around your list of clients and each of the views or screens pertaining to that client's information. The functions for these buttons are also available under Tools from the pull-down menus. If you look at the pull-down options under Tools, you'll also see the other shortcuts available using the keyboard to perform these same functions. When you have completed the Name & Address view, you are ready to move to the next screen, Custom Client Fields.

The combo box above this screen lets you switch from one panel to another within the Client Information screen. You can click on the combo button and select Custom Client Fields to move to the next screen. Version 8 changes the look with Windows 95-style tabs instead of pick lists. The functions, for the most part, are similar to earlier versions. You could also click on the Cycle button at the bottom of the tool buttons on the right-hand side, use the option under Tools on the pull-down menus for Next View, or you can press the **F6** function key to bring you to the next screen.

Attaching Custom Client Fields to Client's Information Screen

You may recall that you defined these fields under **Settings** (See page 128. Now, you are ready to associate information for them as your default. When you set up your actual clients, you will attach the information to those records. Depending on how many custom client fields you have created, you will have either one or two Custom Fields panels. In Your Company, you want to enter the most common answers to each of these questions. If the senior partner is responsible for bringing in most of the new business in the firm, you would want to select him or her as the Billing Attorney. If you see only Controller and Salutation, you should read the section "How to Create Custom Client Fields" on page 129 to define custom client fields. You can override any of these for a particular client or a particular matter.

You can skip most of the remaining panels for Your Company, since options like flat-fee arrangements are typically selected on a client-by-client basis.

Tax, Interest & Markup

If your firm wants to have Timeslips round your time to the nearest tenth of an hour or is charging interest, you should move to the Tax, Interest & Markup view. On the right-hand side, you need to let Timeslips know that it should round your time to the nearest six minutes.

If your firm charges interest for most or all of your clients, you should enter your rate and arrangement here. If you only charge interest for selected clients, you should this information directly on those client's information screens.

Press the cycle button on the right side or the **F6** key until you get to Bill Format 1 View.

Bill Format 1 and 2

The Bill Format views 1 and 2 are used to help define the specific information from your slips and client information that appear on your actual bills. This will ultimately be done on a client-by-client basis or matter-by-matter basis depending on your particular bill options. The information you should select for Your Company's screen should be the bill format that you use in most circumstances. One of the most common formats that law firms use is shown below in Figure 43.

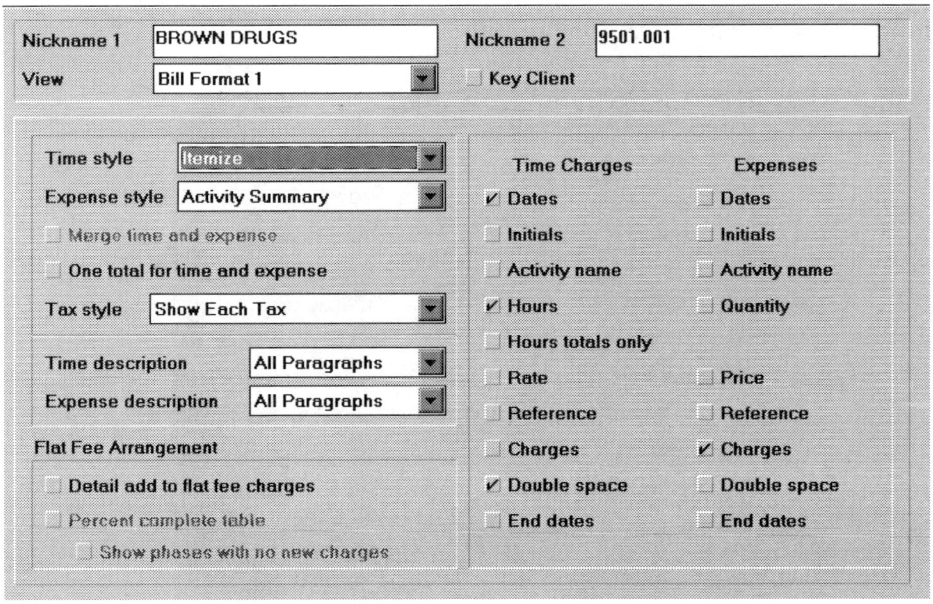

FIGURE 43. Client Information: Bill Format 1 View

MM/DD/YY	This is where the description for each timeslip will appear as it was entered into the program.	.2
MM/DD/YY	This is where more description for each timeslip will appear as it was entered into the program.	.3

	.5 $150.00
Fax Charges	$2.50
Postage	$2.90

If you have several timekeepers working on the case, you may also wish to select initials under the Time column so that you can print the attorney's initials next to each of their slips.

For more information on these options, refer to the Chapter 5, Getting More Professional-Looking Bills.

Bill Format 2

Most of the options on this screen (see Figure 44) should apply to all of your firm's client bills. Ideally, you should show payments, credits, refunds, and prior balance on your bills.

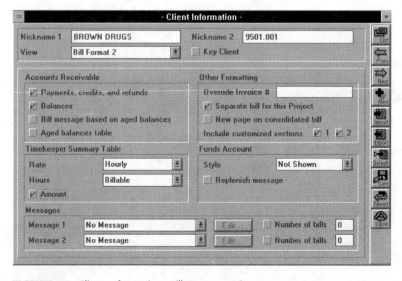

FIGURE 44. Client Information: Bill Format 2 View

The user summary table can give you a recap of who did work, their hourly rate, the number of hours, and their amount. Its precise location on the bill is determined under the Section/Order and Attributes portion of the Bill Layout. Below is an example of a summary table:

Attorney Summary

Attorney	**Hours**	**Rate**	**Amount**
Carol L. Schlein, Partner	5.1	$200.00	$1,020.00
Lee Jefferies, Legal Assistant	4.0	90.00	360.00

If this is something that you want to include on most or all of your bills, you should select this under Your Company so that it gets pulled in as the default or preset option for new clients or cases as you set them up.

On the right-hand side of this screen you will see a field, Starting Invoice Number. Your Company is the only client that has Starting Invoice Number in this location. If you want Timeslips to generate unique invoice numbers, use this field to designate your starting number. As you process a group of bills, this number will automatically increment in sequence for each of those bills.

The Separate Bill for this Project and New page on Consolidated Bill refer back to the Key Client options discussed on page 116. If you are using the Key Client option, and prefer to have separate bills for each matter, you should make sure that the Separate Bill box is checked. If, however, you wish to have a consolidated bill, where all the bills for each matter for a selected Key Client are grouped together, and you want the option to create a summary page but you want each bill to start on a new page, you should check the other option, New page on Consolidated Bill.

The Bill Format is one of four parts of the program that determine what the actual bill for a given client or matter will look like. The Bill Layout, which is discussed in Chapter 5, Getting More Professional Looking Bills, determines both the structure and some other specific formatting issues concerning the bill. The chapter on bill layout also includes sample bills with the information about which options were used to prepare them.

The Include Customized sections here refers to options available on the bill layout itself. Customize Section 1 allows you to have custom information in *front* of a bill. This may be used, for instance, for a cover page with summary information. Customize Section 2 is preset to print at the *end* of a bill. You can select fields from any portion of the database to be included in either of these customized sections. Under Order and Attributes within the Bill Layout program itself, you can also select where on the bill you want these particular components to appear as well as where you would like the attorney summary table to appear if you are using it.

Funds Account is what is used to manage retainer and escrow-type trust transactions that you need to keep segregated from actual payments received from your client. If you are using this option, you may wish to switch style from "Not Shown" to either "itemize" or "summarize."

Most firms do not rely on Timeslips to handle trust or retainer accounts exclusively. In fact, for small firms, unless they have to allocate trust funds to third parties, I recommend that within Timeslips they treat retainer payments as payments, but change the description of the text. If there is money left in the "retainer" account, the bill will show a credit balance. You can tie this to the bill messages and have a credit balance message that says, "No payment due at this time." This is explained on page 40 and in Chapter 6 Special Handling: Flat Fees and Retainers.

When you have completed Your Company's settings to your satisfaction, you can save these options. To do this you can either click on the **Save** button on the right-hand side, press **CTRL+S,** or use the short cut key **CTRL+W**, which attempts to bring you back to the main Navigator screen. If you have made changes, it will ask you along the way, "Do you want to save these changes?" Reply yes.

Override Client Rates

On the Rates view of each client's information screen, you can let Timeslips know what rate to use for each timekeeper or client. (See Figure 45)

Override rate defaults were added with Timeslips Deluxe Version 6. This, in essence, allows you to create a set of rules for when and under what circumstances you want to override the rates already associated with this client. The overrides can have rules associated with them based on the timekeeper or activity code or both. So, for instance, you could have a completely different rate schedule for in-court activities versus outside-of-court activities. To set this up, you would need to define more activities and group them in such a way as to identify those activities that are associated with work performed in the office and those that are typically performed in connection with court appearances. Another way this feature could be used is to charge a higher billable rate for work performed either by the lawyers or staff outside the normal working hours. Again, you would need to define appropriate activities to have the override rules apply.

Setting Up Timeslips **139**

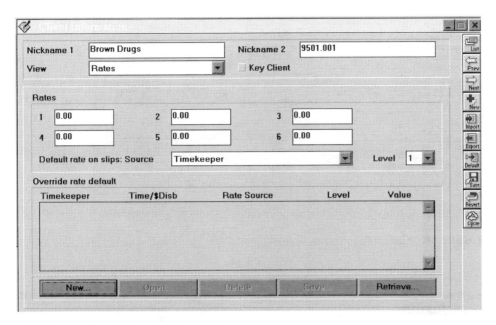

FIGURE 45. Client Information: Rates View

To set up an override rate, select New. The Override Rates Default screen allows you to decide which timekeeper(s) and which activities you want associated with this override rate. For example, you might create an override rate for each litigator in the firm when the activity they work on is "In Court." The bottom half of the screen lets you determine what rate you want in effect. You can select a rate already associated with the attorney or the activity or you can select override from the list and assign a rate. This last option is useful if your firm has a single billing rate for in-court work regardless of which attorney is handling the matter. See Figure 46.

You may have noticed there are two "save" buttons on the screen once you have created your override. The one on the right-hand side of the screen will simply save this client's information screen. The one at the bottom of the screen lets you save your override rate definitions from this screen as a template that you can use for other clients. You might call your template "In Court."

The retrieve option allows you to associate an existing set of override rate defaults with other clients. Go to the other client's rate screen and retrieve the "In Court" template and these special rates will be in effect when the appropriate activity is selected on time slips.

Save any changes before you leave Client Information.

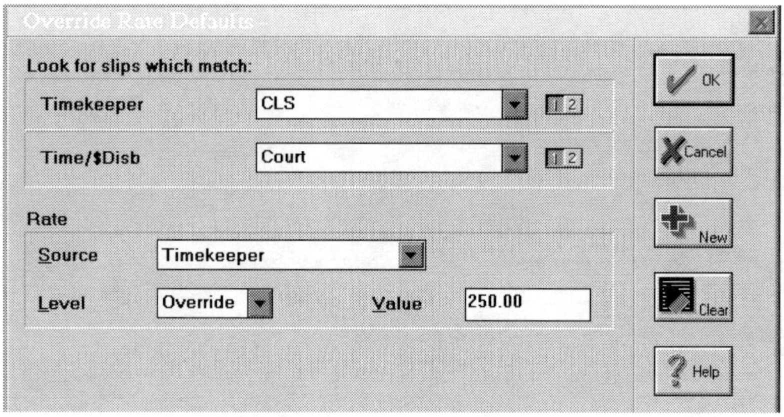

FIGURE 46. Override Rate Defaults Screen

Conclusion

If you follow these steps in setting up Timeslips, you will be able to save a lot of time while using the program to enter your time, expenses, and payments and generating your bills. Some parting advice about the program. If you feel like you are doing something the long way, you should contact a Timeslips guru or Timeslips tech support to determine if there is a faster way to perform the steps. While generally not for beginners, Timeslips includes tools such as Mass Update and Import and Export, which let you work with a group of slips or clients at once rather than one record at a time.

You are now ready to start entering your time, expenses, and payments and get on the road to riches!

APPENDIX **A**

Shortcut Keys

In addition to the menus and the Navigator, Timeslips has many shortcuts available through function keys and Windows shortcut keys. Function keys (the ones with the F and a number, usually located across the top of the keyboard) will be indicated as **F3**. After the function key, the description of the function will appear in French brackets, e.g., {CREATE}.

There is one magical key when working with Timeslips: **CTRL+W** is the shortcut to close all open windows and return to the Main Navigator screen. While it will not work from all submenus, it will work in most and can be very handy. To see it in action, select the Browse Client Information button from the Bill Cycle Navigator panel, then choose a client and open to the Name and Address view. At this point, you will have two windows open. Without **CTRL+W**, you would have to close two separate windows to return to the Main Navigator screen. Pressing **CTRL+W** gets you there quicker. If you have made changes to the client's settings, it will even give you the opportunity to save your changes.

The chart below highlights the most useful of the cursor shortcut keys that are available in Timeslips along with a brief description. The Menu command shortcuts are alternatives to choosing items from the pull-down menus.

The Menu command shortcuts enable you to execute Timeslips menu commands with built-in accelerator keys. Tool shortcuts enable you to execute commands from the Tools menu or the toolbar with built-in accelerator keys. These commands can only be executed when the Tools menu or the tool bar is visible.

KEYSTROKE	DESCRIPTION
\multicolumn{2}{c}{Menu Shortcut Keys}	
Alt+F4	Exit
Ctrl+A	Select all text
Ctrl+B	Generate Bills
Ctrl+C	Copy selected text
Ctrl+F	Full Detail Worksheets
Ctrl+I	Client Information
Ctrl+M	Make Slips
Ctrl+T	Client Transactions (payments, adjustments)
Ctrl+U	Browse Timekeeper (User) Information
Ctrl+V	Paste
Ctrl+W	Close All Windows except Navigator
Ctrl+X	Cut
Ctrl+Y	Browse Activity Information
Ctrl+Z	Undo edit
Ctrl+Del	Delete
F7	Abbreviations
Tool Shortcuts	
Alt+Delete	Delete
Ctrl+E	New Expense
Ctrl+L	List
Ctrl+N	New
Ctrl+N	New Time
Ctrl+O	Open
Ctrl+S	Save
Ctrl+PgDn	Last Record
Ctrl+PgUp	First Record
PgUp	Previous Record
PgDn	Next Record
Esc	Revert or Undo
F6	Cycle between views (Client Information, Billing Assistant, and panels of the Navigator)
Shift+F6	Reverse cycle between views (Client Information, Billing Assistant, and panels of the Navigator)
Make Slips Shortcuts	
Alt+F5[1]	Mark/unmark for deletion

Alt+F8	Clone Rest of Slip
Alt+F9	Summary information
Alt+F10	Turn off all Timers
Alt+Ins	Insert Private Text Indicator
Alt+Shift+D	Insert current date in Description
Alt+Shift+M	Insert current time in Description
Ctrl+D	Duplicate Entire Slip
Ctrl+E or Ctrl+F3	New Expense Activity Code if Activity List is open
Ctrl+N	New Time Activity Code is Activity List is open
Ctrl+F	Search criteria
Ctrl+G or F2	Go To Slip
Ctrl+L	Display Slip List
Ctrl+M	Turn on Miniview
Ctrl+N or F3	New slip
Ctrl+S	Save slip
Ctrl+T or F5	Turn Timer on/off
Ctrl+X	Maximize Miniview
Ctrl+PgUp	First slip
Ctrl+PgDn	Last slip
PgUp	Previous slip
PgDn	Next slip
Esc	Revert or undo
F4	Expand/Contract drop-down list
F6	Next Panel
F8	Clone Field
F9	Show pop-up menu next to a field
Date Shortcut Options in Make Slips and Select Screens	
T	Today's Date
S	Same as Other
>	Add day
<	Subtract day
"+"	Add days
"-"	Subtract days
S	Time Spent: Start/Stop Duration
"+"	Time Spent: Add time
"-"	Time Spent: Subtract time

[1]Alt+F5 only works if the DOS-compatible keyboard is enabled

APPENDIX B

Basic Procedures Checklist for Timeslips Deluxe for Windows

- ✓ Define any new attorneys, clients, or activities
  [Names: Client Info; Names: Timekeeper Info; Names: Activity Info]
- ✓ During the month, enter time slips, disbursements.
  [Slips: Make Slips or New Slip or CTRL+M or TSTIMER icon]
- ✓ Enter any payments.
  [Names: Client Transactions or Browse Client Info, Transactions]
- ✓ Back up Your Data Each Day You Enter New Information Into Timeslips.

  Be sure to back up on something other than your hard disk (e.g. diskettes or a tape drive). A good system is to have ODD and EVEN day sets—ODD for odd-numbered days; EVEN for even-numbered days.
- ✓ Print the Detail Listing or User Defined Slip Analysis Report and Transaction Report as needed to verify the information entered into the system.
  [Reports: Slip Analysis, Detail Listing and Reports: Client, Transaction Listing]
- ✓ At the end of the month, print BILLING WORKSHEETS and distribute them to the attorneys for editing and bill text.
  [Bills: Pre-Bill Worksheets, Full Detail]

- ✓ Edit slips and create summary slips as indicated on the edited Billing Worksheets using Billing Assistant
  [Bills: Billing Assistant]
- ✓ BACK UP YOUR DATA.
- ✓ Print Bills, then Finalize. Optionally, you can place bills on Proof Stage until bills are perfect and use Revision Stage to revise bills on Proof Stage.
  [Bills: Generate Bills]
- ✓ Print any Timeslip or Client Reports necessary (e.g. Client Name & Address Listing, Accounts Receivable, etc.) depending on your firm's preference, these may be done *before* or *after* finalizing. If after, be sure to select Include Billed Items.
- ✓ Before printing Worksheets for next billing cycle or once per quarter, Close billed slips.
  [Slips: Close Slips]

APPENDIX C

Timeslips Reports

Source: Help Files in Timeslips Deluxe   © Copyright Timeslips Corporation

SLIP ANALYSIS

Uses the information entered on the time and expense slips—names, dates, charges, descriptions and status. They do not include information from the Client Information screens or transaction records or client information included on bills and worksheets.

DETAIL LISTING	Prints nearly every piece of information that appears on a slip in detail. This report cannot be summarized, but it can contain subtotaled amounts.
USER SUMMARY	Summarizes the slip information and offers analysis of hours and dollars for users. Displays both billable and unbillable totals and percent of grand totals for most items. Can be displayed as text or as graph.
CLIENT SUMMARY	Summarizes the slip information and offers analysis of hours and dollars for clients. Displays both billable and unbillable totals and percent of grand totals for most items. Can be displayed as text or as graph.
ACTIVITY SUMMARY	Summarizes the slip information and offers analysis of hours and dollars for clients. Displays both billable and unbillable totals and percent of grand totals for most items. Can be displayed as text or as graph.

USER DEFINED	Lists fields specified for each slip included in the report. Can include any field from the time or expense slip. Only fields that provide totaling information may be included in the summary format. Many of the fields can be printed in a variety of formats. Can be sorted and subtotaled to provide further information. Can be saved as a comma-delimited file that can be imported into other applications, such as spreadsheets or databases.
PERIODIC TOTALS	Shows totals for hours, fees, and costs for slips in a periodic table. May show daily, weekly, monthly, quarterly, semiannual, or yearly totals. Depending on the sort, may display totals for users, clients, or activities, can use frames and gridlines to make the report easier to read.
PRODUCTIVITY ANALYSIS	Shows a periodic table of hours, fees, and costs comparing billable and unbillable amounts. The percentage billable of each total is also displayed.
PROFITABILITY ANALYSIS	Displayed in a periodic table. Compares the amounts on the slips to the amount actually billed and shows the difference and percent difference between slip and billed totals.

CLIENT

Client reports compile data from the Client Information, Transactions, History, and Client References dialog boxes. Unlike Slip Analysis Reports, Bills and Worksheets reports, and Client WIP reports, Client Reports do not include information directly from slips.

NAME & ADDRESS LISTING	Gives an address list with phone numbers, in reference to text, and client notes. The primary or secondary nickname, as determined by the sort order, will also be included.
LABELS	Can print various label styles for mailing, Rolodex cards, file folders, and envelopes. Can change the definition and names of the preset styles and add additional styles. The structure of the label report is controlled by

	choosing the Template button from the settings in the dialog box.
ACCOUNTS RECEIVABLE	Provides analysis of overdue balances, broken down by the aging periods defined in the Financial Settings dialog box. Includes payments and payments from the client funds accounts, but does not include any unbilled slips or charges.
TRANSACTION LISTING	Prints transactions with totals. For each transaction listed, the report includes the client nickname (as determined by the sort order), date of the transaction, description, and amount. This report can be subtotaled by client, transaction date, or custom field.
CLIENT FUNDS	Prints information based on client funds transactions (payments from account, withdrawals from account, payments to account, and deposits to account), optionally including a starting balance and ending balance. Can also print a running total, displaying the total after each separate transaction. Use the selection options to exclude clients with a zero balance, or include billed transactions.
HISTORY LISTING	Prints the contents of the Client History dialog box for each client. Cumulative totals for the current fiscal period and since inception are shown with the monthly totals for payments and invoices in the past twelve months. A total of all selected clients prints at the end of the report. Option to include unbilled payments. Enables you to clear totals for the current fiscal period.
MONTHLY TOTALS	Lists payments against invoices for each client selected on a monthly basis. Shows monthly grand totals, subtotals by custom client field (when using that sort criterion), and optional totals for clients with multiple projects. Option to include unbilled payments. Data is taken from the Monthly Totals column in the Client History dialog box. Since each month

	included in the report adds another column, may have to access by using a DOS editor (if the report is printed to a file using Report format), by using landscape printing or a smaller font.
REFERENCE LISTING	Shows the reference codes and their descriptions assigned to each client. Can be sorted by the primary or secondary nicknames, or by one of the custom fields.
USER DEFINED	Lists fields you specify for each client selected. Can include any field from client information, client history and client budgets. Many of the fields can be printed in a variety of formats. Can also be saved as a comma-delimited file that can be imported into other applications, such as spreadsheets or databases.
NICKNAME LISTING	Prints the nicknames, rate table, and reference names for every client in the database. The default rate source and rate level are also included.
HIDDEN NICKNAME LISTING	For each hidden client, prints the primary and secondary nicknames, and the date that the client was hidden.
OVERRIDE RATE LISTING	Prints the override rate defaults for each selected client. These rate defaults are defined in the Rates view of the Client Information dialog box.

CLIENT WIP

Takes information from client information and history and adds it to work in progress as recorded on your slips.

BUDGET	Compares the actual hours, fees, and costs to the budget amounts entered in the Client Budgets dialog box. You may compare budgeted amounts against the original slip values or the billed slip values.
BUDGET BREAKDOWN BY USER	Compares the actual hours, fees, and costs to the user-specific budgets entered in the Client Budgets dialog box. You may compare budgeted amounts against the original slip values or the billed slip values.

BUDGET BREAKDOWN BY ACTIVITY	Compares the actual hours, fees, and costs to the activity-specific budgets entered in the Client Budgets dialog box. You may compare budgeted amounts against the original slip values or the billed slip values.
BUDGET BREAKDOWN BY REFERENCE	Compares the actual hours, fees, and costs to the reference-specific budgets entered in the Client Budgets dialog box. You may compare budgeted amounts against the original slip values or the billed slip values.
CHARGES ON HOLD	Prints the total of time and expense charges on hold. Values are taken both from slips with a hold status and slips that are affected by the hold options of the Flat Fee & Hold view of the Client Information dialog box.
FLAT FEE PERFORMANCE	Evaluates flat fees set up for each client. Compares flat-fee charges with the actual slip charges to determine the profitability of the flat fee. Current and completed flat fees are included. Optionally use the historical values for the current fiscal period or since inception for comparisons.
AGED CLIENT INVESTMENT	Ages work in progress and accounts receivable balances and provides a total of the two balances, along with each balance's percentage of the total. Used to track your financial exposure.
AGED WIP	Breaks down unbilled slips into user-defined aging periods to help identify clients who have generated charges that have not been billed. Optionally details the fees and costs for each client, shows the percentage of the total for each value, and prints the report using a grid.
PRODUCTIVITY BY RATE	Provides analysis of each client rate level. It identifies each rate that has appeared on slips, and lists the rates from the rate table at specified levels, overridden rates, and flat charge slips. Compares billable versus unbillable hours and fees and computes the billable percentage. Computes the average

billing rate by dividing the billable dollars by the billable hours.

USER (TIMEKEEPER)

Analyzes data from the user name list. These reports provide information on rates, history, and other data taken from user information and user history. Unbilled slips are included in some reports for up-to-the-minute analysis. All User Reports may be sorted by either the primary or secondary user nickname.

NICKNAME LISTING	Prints the primary and secondary nicknames, rate table, overhead rate, initials, and full name for every user in the database. Each field is taken from the User Information dialog box.
HISTORY ANALYSIS	Evaluates information in the User History dialog box to show how much of the time and fees of each user is actually charged. Shows totals of billable hours and fees. Billable hours and fees are compared to total hours and billed fees.
ADJUSTMENT HISTORY	Prints adjustment history for each user, including fee, cost, and total bill adjustments that have been billed. Includes adjustments assigned directly to the user and prorated amounts from adjustments allocated to all users. Write-up and write-down totals for fees, costs, and total bill are included for the current fiscal period (YTD) and the history since the user's inception (ITD), as well as a net adjustment total.
OVERALL HISTORY	Merges amounts from the User History Analysis and User Adjustment History reports. Displays billable and unbillable totals for hours. Billable fees and billed fees are included with the net adjustment total (the net of write ups and write downs). These amounts are calculated for the current fiscal period (YTD) and the history since the user's inception (ITD).
USER CONTRIBUTION	Provides an up-to-the-minute look at and the percentage of unbilled and billed hours and fees. Includes hours and fees that have not

	yet appeared on bills (WIP). Expense slips are not included. You may choose the source for the billed information, from the current fiscal period, or from the history since inception.
PRODUCTIVITY BY RATE	Provides analysis of each user rate level. Identifies each rate that has appeared on slips, and lists the rates from the rate table at specified levels, overridden rates, and flat-charge slips. Compares billable versus unbillable hours and fees and computes the billable percentage. It computes the average billing rate by dividing the billable dollars by the billable hours.
OVERHEAD COST	Shows the amount each user is to be paid (based on the user's overhead rate), the amount billed for each user, and the difference and percentage difference between the two amounts. Presented in a periodic format, showing totals within a certain period of time, such as weekly, monthly, or quarterly.

ACTIVITY

Provides information on rates and markup adjustments, and some include unbilled slips to give an up-to-the-minute analysis. May be sorted by either the primary or secondary activity nickname.

NICKNAME LISTING	Prints the primary and secondary nicknames, rate table, tax and markup information, slip defaults, and full name for every time activity and expense in the database. Each field is taken from the Activity Information dialog box.
MARKUP ANALYSIS	Summarizes the total markup or markdown for both billed and unbilled charges. Slip values are totaled per activity, both before and after the effects of the markup. If the source of the markup is from clients (and differs from client to client), the markup percentage is indicated as a calculated figure. Only those activities that exist on slips included in the selection will appear on the report. Can be

	printed to an ASCII-delimited file to export for use with other applications.
PRODUCTIVITY BY RATE	Provides analysis of each activity rate level. Identifies each rate that has appeared on slips, listing the rates from the rate table at specified levels, overridden rates, and flat charge slips. Compares billable versus unbillable hours and fees and computes the billable percentage. Computes the average billing rate by dividing the billable dollars by the billable hours.

SYSTEM REPORTS

ABBREVIATIONS	Prints the abbreviation codes, along with their expanded meanings, for all abbreviations in the database. Interactive prompts are displayed as %prompt% within this list. If personal abbreviations exist, they will print on a separate page after the database abbreviations.
GLOBAL REFERENCE NAMES	Prints the reference code and description for all current entries in the Global References dialog box.
CUSTOM FIELDS	Lists all the custom fields in the database. For each field, lists the field name, type, and for List-type fields, the values of the list.
SLIP FILE CHECK	Reports any errors affecting the currently accessed slip file.
CLIENT FILE CHECK	Reports any errors affecting the Client data files within the currently accessed database.
TIMESLIPS DATABASE CHECK	Reports any errors affecting the data files within the currently accessed database.

TAL OR TAL DELUXE

TAL (Timeslips Accounting Link) Reports available when TAL or TAL Deluxe is installed. TAL and TAL Deluxe are purchased separately from Timeslips Corporation.

TRANSFER REGISTER	Provides a written record of the information that TAL transfers to your general ledger.
INVOICE LISTING	Prints the amounts billed and paid on selected invoices.

WRITE UP/WRITE DOWN	Prints the amount of adjustments applied to selected invoices.
TAXES	Prints the amount of tax billed and paid on selected invoices.
PAYMENT PERFORMANCE	Analyzes how payments are apportioned to users, clients, activities, or user-type custom client fields displayed in your choice of periodic formats, such as by Month or Year.
PAYMENT DISTRIBUTION	Reflects the distribution of payments to various invoices, as allocated at the Apply Payment To Invoices dialog box.
AGED INVOICE	Shows invoices in an aged format, enabling you to quickly identify which need action for collections.
GENERATE STATEMENTS	Can provide your clients with a chronological list of invoices and payments.
CONVERT CASH TO ACCRUAL	Allows you to record amounts owed on existing unpaid invoices when converting from cash to accrual.

Index

Abbreviations, work description, 5–6,
    131–133
  creating, 132
  in time slips, 16
Abbreviations Report, 52, 154
Absolute dates, 18–60
Absolute flat fees, 109, 110
Accounts Receivable Report, 51, 52, 149
Active slips, 31
Activity Codes
  on bills, 77
  creating, 25–27, 122
  on disbursement slips, 25
  on time slips, 16
Activity Nicknames, 52, 124–126
Activity panel, 8, 9
Activity Reports, 52, 153–154
Actual dates, 18, 60
Address, company, 134
Advanced Navigator, 7
Advanced retainers, 105, 106
Aged Client Investment Report, 52, 152
Aged WIP Report, 52, 151
Alternate file paths, 35
Amount field, 39–40
Attorney Overhead Cost Report,
    121, 153
Attorney Reports, 52, 152–153
Attorneys. *See* Users
Automatic Payment, 107

Backup systems, 20, 72
  before finalized bill, 85–86
  need for, 55
  options for, 119
Balances & Funds panel, 106
Base flat fees, 109
Basic Navigator, 7–8

Bill Cycle panel, 8, 9
Bill Format, 54, 92, 137
  Format 1, 69, 92, 135–136
  Format 2, 92, 106, 136–138
Bill Image, 48, 83
Bill Layout. *See* TSLayout
Bill Sort, 65
Bill Sort by Reference, 65
Billing Arrangement Panel, 69
Billing Assistant, 4–5
  corrections with, 67–71
  graphics for, 47–48
Billing cycles. *See also* Bills
  differing, 65
  overview of, 45–51
  reports for. *See* Reports
Billing rates, 120–121
  number of, 54
  overriding, 6, 122, 138–140
  Rate Source, 115–116
Billing Status Options, 21–22
  on expense slips, 27, 29
  on time slips, 19
Billing Worksheets, 51, 63–66
  Full Detail, 46–47, 52–53, 63, 111
  Summary, 49, 51, 78–79
Bills, 51, 56
  adjustments to, 69–70
  backing up, 72, 85–86
  editing, 67–71, 83–84
  finalizing. *See* Finalizing bills
  formats for. *See* Bill Format
  layouts for. *See* TSLayout
  printing, 72–82
  reprinting, 49, 87–89
  review on screen, 48, 80–81
  sample formats for, 98–104
  task-based, 122–124

tips for, 52–55
undoing finalized, 48–49, 86–87
Bookmark, 31
Browse Transaction screen, 38, 41

Calendar, 17, 60
Capacity, 114–115
Cases. *See* Clients
Charges on Hold Report, 46, 52, 62–63, 71, 151
Client Funds, 41–42, 106
Client Funds Report, 112, 149
Client Nicknames, 15–16, 25
Client Reports, 52, 148–150
Client User Defined Report, 56
Client WIP Reports, 52, 112, 150–152
Clients, 3
  on bill, 76–77
  Custom Client Fields for. *See* Custom Client Fields
  defaults for, 134
  hiding, 5
  key, 116–118
  methods for handling, 116–118
  panel, 8, 9
  on payment slip, 39
  as rate source, 115
  setting up, 133
Close Slips, 5
Company address, 134
Contingency flat fees, 109–110
Control options, 35
Custom Client Fields, 63, 64–65, 77
  attaching to Client Information screen, 134
  creation of, 129–131
  fields for, 128–129
Customize sections, 137

Daily Time Report, 46, 56–60
Database, creation of, 113
Date fields, 39, 129, 130
  End Date, 18, 29, 60
  Start Date, 17–18, 29, 60
Deposit retainers, 105
Deposit to Account, 107–108
Description
  abbreviations for, 5–6, 16, 131–133
  on expense slips, 27–28
  on time slips, 16
  for transaction entries, 40
Detail Reports, 20, 57
Disbursement Detail Report, 46

Disbursements
  codes for, 25–27, 126–128
  shortcuts for, 29–30
  slips for, 23–30, 93
Display options, 35

Editing, 30
  bills, 67–71
  expense slips, 68
  payments, 69
  in Slip List, 34
  time slips, 68
End Date, 18, 29, 60
Escrow transactions, 42, 106–109, 138
Expense codes
  entering, 126–128
  setting up, 25–27
Expenses. *See* Disbursements

File maintenance panel, 8, 9
Finalizing bills, 73, 84–86
  purpose of, 48, 49, 82–83
  without Proof Stage, 81–82
Financial Settings, 120
Flat Fee & Hold panel, 70, 109
Flat Fee Performance Report, 52, 112, 151
Flat fees, 69, 109–111
Flat retainers, 105
Fonts, 66
  Font screen, 55, 56
  Settings, 96
Format. *See* Bill Format
From Date field, 17–18, 29
Full Detail Billing Worksheet, 46–47, 51
  tips for, 52–53
  uses of, 63, 111
Funds Account, 138

Go To, 30–31
Guided Tour Navigator, 7

Help, 4, 55
Hold, charges on, 70–71. *See also* Charges on Hold Report
Hold Full Bill, 70–71
Hold on Bill, 70

Icons, 3–4
Import, 4
Interchange Format, 56
Interest, 135
Interface view panel, 118–119

Key clients, 116–118
Keyboard options, 34

Layout. *See* TSLayout
Legal-ABA Litigation Task Codes, 113, 123
Legalgard, 26, 124
Letterhead, 95
List fields, 129, 130–131
List View, 5

Markup, 26, 135
Matters. *See* Clients
Maximum flat fees, 109
Minimum flat fees, 109
Minimum retainers, 105, 106
MiniView, 32
Monthly retainers, 109–111
Monthly Totals Report, 52, 149

Name & Address Listing Report, 52, 148
Navigators
  Navigator Editor, 4
  options for, 119
  panels for, 8–9
  types of, 7–9
Nicknames
  Activity, 52, 124–126
  Attorney, 15, 23–25, 120–121
  Client, 15–16, 25
  as expense activity codes, 25–26
No Detail Worksheets, 51

Online User's Guide, 4
Operational Preferences, 115
Options screen, reports, 55, 78–79, 92–93
  Billing Worksheets, 66
  User Defined Slip Report, 62
Overhead Rate, 121
Override Rates, 6, 138–140

Payment to Account, 107, 108–109
Payments
  adding, 40–41
  Browse Payments, 41
  editing, 69
  entering, 37–40
  retainers as, 105–112
Percent Complete, 110
Personal Preferences, 118–119
Phrases for bill, 96
Preferences, 34–36
  operational, 115
  personal, 118–119

Printing
  bills, 72–80
  copy to file, 81
  to display, 80–81
  procedures, 80–82
  reports, 56, 62, 66
  reprinting, 49, 87–89
Private Text, 114
Profiles, 119
Proof Stage, 50, 73, 82–83

Rate Source, 115–116
Rates. *See* Billing Rates
Read Me, 4
References, 77
  on expense slips, 28–29
  on time slips, 16–17
Relative dates, 18, 60–62
Replenish, 108
Report Format, 56
Report Wizard, 5, 51
Reports, 51–52, 147–155. *See also* specific reports
  printing, 56, 62, 66
  styles of, 57
  uses of, 111–113
Reprint Bills, 48, 87
Restore, 72
Retainers
  Funds Account for, 138
  methods for, 105–109
  monthly, 109–111
  reports for, 111–112
  types of, 105
Retrieving, 59, 62, 78
Revise Date, 74–75
Revision Stage, 6, 50–51, 73, 84

Saving. *See also* Backup systems
  report settings, 59, 62
  slips, 19–20, 29
  transactions, 40
Script Editor, 4
  options, 119
  SCRIPTS.WRI, 4
Search, 31
Security, 119
Select screen, reports, 55, 75–76, 92
  Billing Worksheets, 63, 64–65
  User Defined Slip Report, 59–60
Settings panel, 8, 9
Shortcut keys, 141–143
Slip Analysis Report, 51, 147–148

Slip Defaults, 5, 35, 127
Slip List, 32–34
Slips
  active, 31
  disbursement, 23–32, 93
  duplicating, 30
  editing, 30, 68
  new, 14
  options for, 30–35
  saving, 19–20, 29
  time, 13–22, 93
Sort screen, reports, 55, 78, 92–93
  Billing Worksheets, 63, 65–66
  User Defined Slip Report, 62
Speller, 1, 35
Start Date, 17–18, 29, 60
Summary, 31
Summary reports, 57
Summary Worksheet. *See* Billing
  Worksheets
Supervisor, 119
Systems Reports, 52, 154

Task-based billing, 122–124
Tax, 26, 127, 135
Template, 57
  bill, 79–80
  Template screen, 55, 56
Terminology, 113–114
Text fields, 129, 130
Thru Date, 18, 29
Time and Expense panel, 8, 9
Time slips, 13–22, 93
Time Spent, 18–19
Timekeeper Reports, 52, 152–153
Timekeepers. *See* Users
Timer, 12
  on/off button for, 15, 17
  in Slip List, 34
Timeslips
  advantages of, 1, 12
  help on, 4, 55
  page checklist for, 10–12
  procedures checklist for, 145–146
  setting up, 113–140
  shortcut keys, 141–143
  Version 5 or earlier, 73–74
  Version 6 upgrade, 32, 34, 138
  Version 7 upgrade, 4–6, 31, 32
  Version 8 upgrade, 6–7, 50
Timeslips Accounting Link (TAL), 1,
  39–40, 78, 154–155
Totals Only Worksheets, 51

Transaction Listing Report, 52, 149
Transaction Report, 46
Transactions
  Browse Transaction Screen, 41
  for flat fees and retainers, 106, 107
  panel, 8, 9
  for payments, 38–40
  removing, 41
  types of, 43–44
Troubleshooting Guide, 4
Trust funds, 106
TSIMPORT.WRI, 4
TSLayout, 4, 54, 137
  changing, 93–96
  enhancements to, 6
  font settings for, 96
  order/attributes of, 96–98
  phrases in, 96
  use of, 91–92
TSReport, 3, 13, 37
TSTimer, 3, 13
  DOS icon, 4
  exiting, 20, 36
  for expense slips, 23–36
  shortcuts for, 20–22
  for time slips, 13–22
Tutorial, 4
TWSpell, 4
Type field, 38

Undoing finalized bills, 49, 86–87
Update, 48
User Contribution Report, 112,
  152–153
User Defined Client Report, 52, 150
User Defined Slip Analysis Report, 51,
  56, 57–60, 148
User fields, 129, 130
User Nicknames
  creating, 120–121
  on disbursement slips, 23–25
  Disbursements, 121
  on time slips, 15
User Reports, 52, 152–153
Users, 3
  billing rates for. *See* Billing rates
  panel, 8, 9
  as rate source, 115

Worksheets, billing. *See* Billing
  Worksheets

Your Company screen, 133

Selected Books From...
THE LAW PRACTICE MANAGEMENT SECTION

ABA Guide to Lawyer Trust Accounts. This book deals with how lawyers should manage trust accounts to comply with ethical & statutory requirements.

ABA Guide to Professional Managers in the Law Office. This book shows how professional management can and does work. It shows lawyers how to practice more efficiently by delegating management tasks to professional managers.

Billing Innovations. This book examines how innovative fee arrangements and your approach toward billing can deeply affect the attorney-client relationship. It also explains how billing and pricing are absolutely intertwined with strategic planning, maintaining quality of services, marketing, instituting a compensation system, and firm governance.

Changing Jobs, 2nd Ed. A handbook designed to help lawyers make changes in their professional careers. Includes career planning advice from nearly 50 experts.

Compensation Plans for Law Firms, 2nd Ed. This second edition discusses the basics for a fair and simple compensation system for partners, of counsel, associates, paralegals, and staff.

Computer-Assisted Legal Research: A Guide to Successful Online Searching. Covers the fundamentals of LEXIS®-NEXIS® and WESTLAW®, including practical information such as: logging on and off; formulating your search; reviewing results; modifying a query; using special features; downloading documents.

Connecting with Your Client. Written by a psychologist, therapist, and legal consultant, this book presents communications techniques that will help ensure client cooperation and satisfaction.

Do-It-Yourself Public Relations. A hands-on guide for lawyers with public relations ideas, sample letters and forms. The book includes a diskette that includes model letters to the press that have paid off in news stories and media attention.

Finding the Right Lawyer. This guide answers the questions people should ask when searching for legal counsel. It includes a glossary of legal specialties and the ten questions you should ask a lawyer before hiring.

Flying Solo: A Survival Guide for the Solo Lawyer, 2nd ed. An updated and expanded guide to the problems and issues unique to the solo practitioner.

How to Draft Bills Clients Rush to Pay. A collection of techniques for drafting bills that project honesty, competence, fairness and value.

How to Start and Build a Law Practice, 3rd ed. Jay Foonberg's classic guide has been updated and expanded. Included are more than 10 new chapters on marketing, financing, automation, practicing from home, ethics and professional responsibility.

Visit our Web site:
http//www.abanet.org/lpm/catalog

To order: Call Toll-Free 1-800-285-2221

Law Office Policy and Procedures Manual, 3rd Ed. Provides a model for law office policies and procedures. It covers law office organization, management, personnel policies, financial management, technology, and communications systems. Includes diskette.

The Lawyer's Guide to Creating Web Pages. A practical guide that clearly explains HTML, covers how to design a Web site, and introduces Web-authoring tools.

The Lawyer's Guide to the Internet. A guide to what the Internet is (and isn't), how it applies to the legal profession, and the different ways it can -- and should -- be used.

The Lawyer's Guide to Marketing on the Internet. This book talks about the pluses and minuses of marketing on the Internet, as well as how to develop an Internet marketing plan.

The Lawyer's Quick Guide to Microsoft® Internet Explorer; The Lawyer's Quick Guide to Netscape® Navigator. These two guides offer special introductory instructions on the most popular Internet browsers. Four quick and easy lessons including: Basic Navigation, Setting a Bookmark, Browsing with a Purpose, Keeping What You Find.

The Lawyer's Quick Guide to WordPerfect® 7.0/8.0 for Windows®. This easy-to-use guide offers lessons on multitasking, entering and editing text, formatting letters, creating briefs, and more. Perfect for training, this book includes a diskette with practice exercises and word templates.

Leaders' Digest: A Review of the Best Books on Leadership. This book will help you find the best books on leadership to help you achieve extraordinary and exceptional leadership skills.

Living with the Law: Strategies to Avoid Burnout and Create Balance. This multi-author book is intended to help lawyers manage stress, make the practice of law more satisfying, and improve client service.

Practicing Law Without Clients: Making a Living as a Freelance Lawyer. This book describes the freelance legal researching, writing, and consulting opportunities that are available to lawyers.

Running a Law Practice on a Shoestring. Targeted to the solo or small firm lawyer, this book offers a crash course in successful entrepreneurship. Features money-saving tips on office space, computer equipment, travel, furniture, staffing, and more.

Survival Guide for Road Warriors. A guide to using a notebook computer and combinations of equipment and technology so lawyers can be effective in their office, on the road, in the courtroom or at home.

Through the Client's Eyes. Includes an overview of client relations and sample letters, surveys, and self-assessment questions to gauge your client relations acumen.

Women Rainmakers' 101+ Best Marketing Tips. A collection of over 130 marketing tips suggested by women rainmakers throughout the country. Includes tips on image, networking, public relations, and advertising.

Order Form

Qty	Title	LPM Price	Regular Price	Total
_____	ABA Guide to Lawyer Trust Accounts (5110374)	$ 69.95	$ 79.95	$_____
_____	ABA Guide to Prof. Managers in the Law Office (5110373)	69.95	79.95	$_____
_____	Billing Innovations (5110366)	124.95	144.95	$_____
_____	Changing Jobs, 2nd Ed. (5110334)	49.95	59.95	$_____
_____	Compensation Plans for Lawyers, 2nd Ed. (5110353)	69.95	79.95	$_____
_____	Computer-Assisted Legal Research (5110388)	69.95	79.95	$_____
_____	Connecting with Your Client (5110378)	54.95	64.95	$_____
_____	Do-It-Yourself Public Relations (5110352)	69.95	79.95	$_____
_____	Finding the Right Lawyer (5110339)	19.95	19.95	$_____
_____	Flying Solo, 2nd Ed. (5110328)	59.95	69.95	$_____
_____	How to Draft Bills Clients Rush to Pay (5110344)	39.95	49.95	$_____
_____	How to Start & Build a Law Practice, 3rd Ed. (5110293)	32.95	39.95	$_____
_____	Law Office Policy & Procedures Manual (5110375)	99.95	109.95	$_____
_____	Lawyer's Guide to Creating Web Pages (5110383)	54.95	64.95	$_____
_____	Lawyer's Guide to the Internet (5110343)	24.95	29.95	$_____
_____	Lawyer's Guide to Marketing on the Internet (5110371)	54.95	64.95	$_____
_____	Lawyer's Quick Guide to Microsoft Internet® Explorer (5110392)	24.95	29.95	$_____
_____	Lawyer's Quick Guide to Netscape® Navigator (5110384)	24.95	29.95	$_____
_____	Lawyer's Quick Guide to WordPerfect® 7.0/8.0 (5110395)	34.95	39.95	$_____
_____	Leaders' Digest (5110356)	49.95	59.95	$_____
_____	Living with the Law (5110379)	59.95	69.95	$_____
_____	Practicing Law Without Clients (5110376)	49.95	59.95	$_____
_____	Running a Law Practice on a Shoestring (5110387)	39.95	49.95	$_____
_____	Survival Guide for Road Warriors (5110362)	24.95	29.95	$_____
_____	Through the Client's Eyes (5110337)	69.95	79.95	$_____
_____	Women Rainmakers' 101+ Best Marketing Tips (5110336)	14.95	19.95	$_____

*HANDLING
 $10.00-$24.99 ... $3.95
 $25.00-$49.99 ... $4.95
 $50.00+ $5.95

**TAX
 DC residents add 5.75%
 IL residents add 8.75%
 MD residents add 5%

SUBTOTAL: $_____
*HANDLING: $_____
**TAX: $_____
TOTAL: $_____

PAYMENT

☐ Check enclosed (to the ABA) ☐ Bill Me

☐ Visa ☐ MasterCard ☐ American Express   Account Number:_____

Exp. Date:_____ Signature_____

Name_____
Firm_____
Address_____
City_____ State_____ ZIP_____
Phone number_____

Mail to: ABA Publication Orders   Phone: (800) 285-2221   Fax: (312) 988-5568
          P.O. Box 10892
          Chicago, IL 60610-0892   World Wide Web: http//www.abanet.org/lpm/catalog
                                     Email: abasvcctr@abanet.org

 **CUSTOMER COMMENT FORM**

Title of Book: _____

We've tried to make this publication as useful, accurate, and readable as possible. Please take 5 minutes to tell us if we succeeded. Your comments and suggestions will help us improve our publications. Thank you!

1. How did you acquire this publication:

☐ by mail order ☐ at a meeting/convention ☐ as a gift
☐ by phone order ☐ at a bookstore ☐ don't know
☐ other: (describe) _____

Please rate this publication as follows:

	Excellent	Good	Fair	Poor	Not Applicable
Readability: Was the book easy to read and understand?	☐	☐	☐	☐	☐
Examples/Cases: Were they helpful, practical? Were there enough?	☐	☐	☐	☐	☐
Content: Did the book meet your expectations? Did it cover the subject adequately?	☐	☐	☐	☐	☐
Organization and clarity: Was the sequence of text logical? Was it easy to find what you wanted to know?	☐	☐	☐	☐	☐
Illustrations/forms/checklists: Were they clear and useful? Were there enough?	☐	☐	☐	☐	☐
Physical attractiveness: What did you think of the appearance of the publication (typesetting, printing, etc.)?	☐	☐	☐	☐	☐

Would you recommend this book to another attorney/administrator? ☐ Yes ☐ No

How could this publication be improved? What else would you like to see in it?
_____
_____
_____

Do you have other comments or suggestions? _____
_____

Name _____
Firm/Company _____
Address _____
City/State/Zip _____
Phone _____
Firm Size: _____ Area of specialization: _____

We appreciate your time and help.

Fold

NO POSTAGE
NECESSARY
IF MAILED
IN THE
UNITED STATES

BUSINESS REPLY MAIL
FIRST CLASS   PERMIT NO. 16471   CHICAGO, ILLINOIS

POSTAGE WILL BE PAID BY ADDRESSEE

AMERICAN BAR ASSOCIATION
PPM, 8th FLOOR
750 N. LAKE SHORE DRIVE
CHICAGO, ILLINOIS 60611-9851

Fold

Law Practice Management Section

Membership Application

Access to all these information resources and discounts – for just $3.33 a month!

Membership dues are just $40 a year – just $3.33 a month.
You probably spend more on your general business magazines and newspapers.
But they can't help you succeed in building and managing your practice
like a membership in the ABA Law Practice Management Section.
Make a small investment in success. Join today!

☑ **Yes!** I want to join the ABA Section of Law Practice Management Section and gain access to information helping me add more clients, retain and expand business with current clients, and run my law practice more efficiently and competitively!

Check the dues that apply to you:

❏ $40 for ABA members ❏ $5 for ABA Law Student Division members

Choose your method of payment:

❏ Check enclosed (make payable to American Bar Association)
❏ Bill me
❏ Charge to my: ❏ VISA® ❏ MASTERCARD® ❏ AMEX®

Card No.: _____ Exp. Date: _____

Signature: _____ Date: _____

ABA I.D.*: _____
(* *Please note: Membership in ABA is a prerequisite to enroll in ABA Sections.*)

Name: _____

Firm/Organization: _____

Address: _____

City/State/ZIP: _____

Telephone No.: _____ Fax No.: _____

Primary Email Address: _____

Get Ahead.

ABA Law Practice Management Section

Save time by Faxing or Phoning!

▶ Fax your application to: (312) 988-5820
▶ Join by phone if using a credit card: (800) 285-2221 (ABA1)
▶ Email us for more information at: lpm@abanet.org
▶ Check us out on the Internet: http://www.abanet.org/lpm

750 N. LAKE SHORE DRIVE
CHICAGO, IL 60611
PHONE: (312) 988-5619
FAX: (312) 988-5820
Email: lpm@abanet.org

I understand that Section dues include a $24 basic subscription to Law Practice Management; this subscription charge is not deductible from the dues and additional subscriptions are not available at this rate. Membership dues in the American Bar Association are not deductible as charitable contributions for income tax purposes. However, such dues may be deductible as a business expense.